World Holidays

|edited by
MARILYN MARQUIS **and** SARAH NIELSEN

Hye Lin Choi

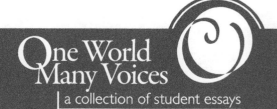

One World Many Voices
|a collection of student essays

No part of this book may be reproduced or transmitted in any form or by any means, electronic or mechanical, including photocopying, recording or by any information storage and retrieval system, without written permission from the author, except for the inclusion of brief quotations in review.

One World Many Voices: World Holidays
Copyright © 2010 by Marilyn Marquis and Sarah Nielsen

All rights reserved.

Published in the United States and the United Kingdom by WingSpan Press, Livermore, CA

The WingSpan name, logo and colophon are the trademarks of WingSpan Publishing.

ISBN 978-1-59594-413-9

First edition 2010

Printed in the United States of America

www.wingspanpress.com

Library of Congress Control Number 2010930632

1 2 3 4 5 6 7 8 9 10

 | **Preface**

This collection of essays, *World Holidays*, is the second book in *One World Many Voices*, a series of collected essays written by and for English language learners. The series stems from an effort to provide easy and interesting extensive reading material for students in the ESL program at Las Positas College, in Livermore, California.

The editors of this series initiated READERS WRITING FOR READERS in 2006 to encourage students to write for readers who are learning English. By participating in READERS WRITING FOR READERS and reading the resulting books, students have the powerful experience of learning from peers and of helping others with their language development. Knowledge comes from students themselves. In reading the writing of their peers, students may simultaneously join a community of readers, discover themselves in the experiences of others, and expand their understanding of the world.

These student-generated essays, edited to control the variety of sentence structure and the range of vocabulary, provide high-beginning level students with interesting, easy to understand material that they can read successfully without the use of a dictionary.

We wish to extend our thanks to the ESL faculty at Las Positas College for engaging their students in READERS WRITING FOR READERS. We are deeply grateful to the students for their genuine and creative contributions.

Marilyn Marquis and Sarah Nielsen, editors

Acknowledgements

WE ARE INDEBTED TO THE students in the English as a Second Language program at Las Positas College for their enthusiastic participation in READERS WRITING FOR READERS. Their heartfelt writing about their lives, their feelings, their families, their customs, and their struggles with living in a new country has inspired us to create this series of student-generated essays for their extensive reading.

We also want to acknowledge many others who have contributed to this series. Fredda Cassidy and the faculty and students in the Visual Communications program at Las Positas College worked patiently with us to establish the look and feel of these books. They designed the layout, logo, and covers through a truly collaborative process, in particular Linda Roberts, Rebecca Schoefer, Melinda Bandler, and Meg Epperly. Thank you!

Thank you also to the instructors in the English as a Second Language program at Las Positas College for inviting us into their classrooms to present READERS WRITING FOR READERS to their students and for encouraging their students to participate in the project.

We would like to acknowledge the contributions of individuals who offered feedback, suggestions, proofreading, and support, with special thanks to Dr. Philip Manwell, Dean of Arts and Communications at Las Positas College.

BOOK TWO — WORLD HOLIDAYS

Table of Contents

The Solar New Year	7
The Lunar New Year	16
Full Moon Festivals	29
Honoring Special People	43
Remembering Ancestors	56
Religious Holidays	68
Christmas in Many Lands	81
Independence Day	98
Unique Holidays	109
Teacher's Guide	127

CHAPTER ONE
The Solar New Year

New Year Celebrations
Brazilian New Year Traditions
The New Year in Peru
The New Year in Russia
A Persian Holiday
Norooz in Afghanistan

The Solar New Year

New Year Celebrations

SARAH NIELSEN

In my family, we didn't have any particular traditions to celebrate the New Year. When I was a small child, I often spent New Year's Eve with my cousins. We tried to stay up until midnight to welcome in the New Year. My aunt always had horns and other noisemakers for us. Sometimes we made it until midnight, and we counted down the last ten seconds of the old year. We cheered and blew our horns when the clock struck twelve. Most of the time, however, we fell asleep long before one year became the next. When I was in my teens and twenties, I usually went to a party with friends to celebrate the New Year. By then, I had seen many movies where people kissed and fell in love as New Year's Eve became New Year's Day. I always imagined I would fall in love with someone on New Year's Eve. It never happened, but I enjoyed imagining it!

Brazilian New Year Traditions

ANONYMOUS

In Brazil, December is considered the best month of the year. Christmas celebrations make this month exciting, but December means great hot weather, the end of one year, and the beginning of a new year.

Before December 31, people go shopping to buy new clothes for the special night. White clothes are traditional for this holiday because white clothes will bring good luck in the coming year. White dresses, shorts, pants, and skirts on the outside hide the symbolic colors underneath. People carefully choose their luck for the coming year with colorful underwear. For example, pink underwear brings love, yellow brings prosperity, and blue brings protection.

Early in the day on December 31, people prepare the midnight meal, the lucky midnight meal. For this occasion, no one eats beef or chicken. Everyone eats pork, usually a whole roasted pig. The meal also includes lentils, rice, and grapes because these are lucky foods. Families and friends gather before midnight to enjoy the meal together and celebrate the coming of the new year.

Fireworks are also a New Year's tradition in Brazil. In Rio de Janeiro, thousands of people gather to watch the spectacular fireworks display, but even in smaller cities and towns, people watch from their homes and apartments, on the beach, or in the streets. After the fireworks are finished, people toast the New Year with champagne. They eat grapes and then hug and kiss. The parties continue on into the night with music and dancing. No one has time for sleep.

Everyone hopes that these traditions will bring a year of peace, luck, and love.

The New Year in Peru
JULIA VASQUEZ

I LIKE THE NEW YEAR CELEBRATION in my country, Peru, because it is so exciting. After Christmas people are looking for a place to say goodbye to the old year and to welcome the New Year. People celebrate in a variety of different places, for example a nightclub, hotel, restaurant, or a house. It all depends on how much money people have to spend. The Peruvians believe that the New Year will be better if it starts in a happy way, and happy means a party with dancing, eating, and enjoying family and friends. The parties should have good music for dancing. Some places contract an orchestra, and others use a stereo with a DJ. The orchestras or DJs play the best songs from that year, and people remember the year through music. There are also colorful decorations. The places are decorated with balloons, paper streamers, and flowers, especially yellow flowers, because Peruvians believe yellow is a lucky color.

To start the New Year, people usually buy new clothes and shoes for the celebration. People choose clothes and shoes according to their style, but almost everyone chooses underwear very carefully. Peruvians wear yellow underwear if they want a lucky year They choose red underwear if they want passion in the year. Peruvians believe in some other traditions to bring a good year. For example, if people want to travel that year, they should run around their neighborhood with their luggage. If they want a lucky year, they should make a circle with salt in their home. Additionally, if someone wants to make a wish, he or she should eat twelve grapes, one for each month.

Food for the New Year's celebration is similar to the food for Christmas. We have dinner with turkey or pork, rice, stuffing, salad, and dessert. Although the food is the same, the celebration is very different. The New Year's celebration happens late on December 31 and continues into the early morning of January First. After having our parties, we take a short nap, and then everybody goes to the beach to enjoy the rest of the day.

I have wonderful memories of New Year's celebrations in Peru.

The New Year in Russia
ELENA MORRIS

NEW YEAR IS THE MOST important and favorite holiday in Russia. This holiday unites all Russians in one big celebration. The traditionally religious holiday of Christmas was banned by the Bolsheviks shortly after the revolution in 1917, so the New Year celebration became very important and cherished. Modern Russia revived the traditional religious roots of Christmas and celebrates New Year only to mark the coming of the next year.

New Year is considered a family holiday, and it is celebrated at home with family members and near and dear friends. In the popular belief, however, people greet the New Year in the way they hope to live in the new year. For this reason, people greet this holiday with a delicious meal and lots of champagne and vodka. Everyone has a traditional fir tree decorated with many ornaments. Under the fir tree is a place for presents and toys delivered by kind Grandfather Frost and his granddaughter the snow maiden.

On December 31, New Year's Eve, at exactly midnight the Russian president delivers his address to the Russian people, and at the Kremlin in Moscow, the clock strikes twelve times. People fill their glasses with sparking champagne and make a wish for what they want to have or see happen during the approaching year. Everybody feels this holiday is special. And when the day is over, everyone has to wait for a whole year until the next magical new year.

A Persian Holiday
MOJDEH KHOSRAVAN

THE MOST CELEBRATED PERSIAN HOLIDAY is called Norooz. Every Norooz, on March 20, 21, or 22, the Persian people celebrate the vernal equinox. This is the very first day of spring and the beginning of the New Year. They believe when winter is over and spring is on the way, every living thing in the world starts a new life. They want to celebrate this new life by spending time with their families and friends and with special food.

In preparation for a new life and the holiday, people clean their houses by washing windows and carpets, painting the walls, preparing the garden for spring, and buying new things for their homes. They throw away any damaged or useless items in the house and replace them with new ones. This takes a long time, so they start preparing a month before the holiday.

The day before Norooz every Persian housewife is very busy cooking different meals for the next day. They prepare grilled chicken, fish, rice and vegetables, and different kinds of stew. They set a big table full of the most delicious food, fruit, and sweets, with candles burning and flowers placed in the middle. Often there is a mirror to symbolize the importance of reflecting on life and a goldfish bowl to symbolize life. There are many special symbolic decorations for Norooz. Seven items all beginning with the letter *s* in Farsi are placed on the table. All these seven things have a special meaning for the coming year. For example, the word apple is *sib* in Farsi. Since *sib* starts with *s*, usually there is a plate full of apples on the table. There are other symbolic foods. Vinegar symbolizes patience; sumac berries symbolize warmth; garlic symbolizes good health; coins symbolize wealth; sugar symbolizes a sweet life; and germinating wheat symbolizes new life.

Children are also very excited about Norooz. They wear their new clothes and receive gifts from the elders. Schools are closed for several days, and there are a lot of TV shows to watch. There are parties everywhere, and families gather together for the happiest time of the year. This is the best time for people to connect with their relations. They gather together and put aside past problems.

I especially miss my country when Norooz is approaching. I won't be able to be home at that time. This is hard, but inevitable. So instead, I try to enjoy holidays here, as much as I can.

Norooz in Afghanistan
ANONYMOUS

THE FIRST DAY OF THE New Year in many eastern countries, such as Afghanistan, Iran, Pakistan, Turkey, Iraq, India, and Azerbaijan, is called Norooz. In these countries, people celebrate Norooz differently. In my native country Afghanistan, people celebrate Norooz for thirteen days. It's a long vacation.

Norooz in Afghanistan is a religious celebration and a New Year celebration. On this day the Holy Prophet Mohammed moved from Mecca to Medina. This was a big event in Islamic history. We celebrate this day because it's a happy and peaceful day for us. We also celebrate the leadership of Imam Ali, who was the second most important person after the Holy Prophet. Imam Ali was kind, brave, just, wise, and tolerant among the people in society. After the Holy Prophet, he knew about what societies need most. Because of this, we have great respect for him and his deeds.

The most important reason that we celebrate Norooz is that it is the new day of nature. On this day, nature comes to life again. We can see some signs of this life everywhere in nature. The night before Norooz, we make cookies and other special sweet foods. On the day of Norooz, when the sun rises, people crowd in the center of the city of Kabul and also in Mazare Sharif, where Imam Ali's shrine is. Fourteen powerful men pick up a special heavy object called *Alam*. If the *Alam* is picked up easily, that means the next year will be a good, peaceful, and successful year for Afghanistan. If it goes the other way, if the *Alam* is hard to pick up, people will have lots of difficulties. Also in the *Alam* ceremony, people pray and ask God (Allah) for forgiveness, guidance, a good life, health, and peace. People thank God for everything.

After that, people congratulate each other on the New Year, Norooz. First, we visit our elderly relatives. Then young people go to the park or the cinema. We dress in our new favorite clothes for Norooz, and we have special Norooz tournaments with different kinds of local sports. One of them is called *Bozkashi*. *Bozkashi* is two groups of strong powerful men, lawfully fighting for one goat. It's so amazing and interesting to see.

We have lots of fun during the thirteen days of Norooz vacations, but on the last day, Siisda Bader, everybody spends time in nature at a park, in the mountains, or in the forest. People make food and cookies, and they eat outside in nature. It's so enjoyable. Also on this day, young women who have never been married spend lots of time in nature and get introduced to young men. They hope to find the proper partner.

In different countries, people celebrate Norooz in different ways based on their own traditions. Norooz for people in Afghanistan and for Afghans everywhere is a very happy, fun, interesting, and holy day.

CHAPTER TWO
The Lunar New Year

The Most Popular Festival
The Most Important Chinese Holiday
Tsagaan Sar in Mongolia
Chinese New Year in Indonesia
Lunar New Year
The Excitement of Tet
Sol-nal in Korea

The Lunar New Year

The Most Popular Festival
HONG ZHANG

CHINESE NEW YEAR IS THE most important and popular of all Chinese festivals. People celebrate with a sacrifice to gods and to their ancestors at the end of the old year and the beginning of the New Year. For this traditional holiday, people prepare for a long time because they will celebrate for fifteen days. With the Chinese lunar calendar, the holiday begins with the new moon on the first day of the lunar New Year and ends on the fifteenth day with the full moon and the Lantern Festival.

Every family purchases some special food for the New Year, such as meat, vegetables, fruit, candies and different kinds of nuts. Also, they buy decorations for their home, new clothes and shoes for children, and gifts for their parents, elderly relatives, and friends. Before the New Year comes, my family cleans and decorates our home. We paste spring festival poetic couplets on each side of the door. We write these in calligraphy on special red paper. We also paste the Chinese character *fu* upside down on the middle of the door. The upside down *fu* means wishes for a bright future and good luck for the New Year. Also, we raise a red lantern over the door, and we hang some Chinese knot decorations in the living room. The color red is everywhere during the New Year celebration because it represents good luck.

Chinese New Year's Eve is of great importance. At that time, all family members come together to see in the New Year together. This is a time of family reunions. In the afternoon, my family prepares a feast with special foods. The dishes always include chicken and fish because chicken means prosperity, and fish means abundance, riches, and togetherness. The family usually sets a place for deceased relatives to honor generations of the past and the present. After the reunion, we sit together chatting and watching TV or playing Mahjong. We stay up to welcome the New Year in at midnight. When the New Year bell rings, the firecracker sounds are soaring. The loud sounds help drive evil spirits away. Everybody says, "Happy New Year" to each other. Adults give a red envelope with lucky money to children for the New Year. When people wake up on the first day of the New Year, they eat dumplings and wish for money and treasure. The shape of the dumplings is like a gold ingot from ancient China and represents good fortune.

During the two week New Year festival, a lively atmosphere fills the streets and lanes. There are many customs for different days during the fifteen-day celebration. People bring gifts to their relatives and friends and wish each other Happy New Year. They visit the temples and eat traditional foods. In addition, many activities such as lion dancing, dragon lantern dancing, lantern festivals and temple fairs will be held until the Lantern Festival marks the end of the New Year festivities.

The Most Important Chinese Holiday
ANDREW LI

EACH HOLIDAY IN CHINA IS meaningful and has a special position in Chinese culture. However, the most important holiday to Chinese people is the Chinese New Year. The favorite ways that many Chinese celebrate this holiday are to cook delicious food, to set off fireworks, and to share this meaningful day with the whole family.

The typical food for Chinese New Year is the dumpling, which is a kind of traditional Chinese food. It is a really delicious food to eat, but it is a very complex food to cook. Therefore, to cook dumplings one needs the whole family to work together. This work isn't just for one or two persons, but every family member. Although the work may seem boring and tedious to outsiders, the family members don't have those feelings. When they are cooking, they talk with each other and share happiness with each other. When they are eating, they share delicious food with each other and have a wonderful time together. The meaning of cooking is not only making delicious food, but also sharing happiness and wonderful times with the whole family. Actually, the activity of cooking displays the true meaning of the holiday.

On Chinese New Year's Day, setting off fireworks is an essential activity. There is an interesting legend about fireworks. A long time ago, an evil monster lived in a mountain. The monster would go out of the mountain and destroy countries and cities every few days. Many people died because of the monster's attacks. Although people tried many ways to defeat the monster, they failed. One day, a smart boy created fireworks. He used fireworks to attack the monster when the monster intruded on his village. The monster was afraid of the loud sound and the strong light that fireworks made. Therefore, the monster left in fear. That day was the first time that people defeated the monster, so people celebrated their success and made that meaningful day into a holiday, the Chinese New Year. Thanks to the fireworks, the monster never showed his face again. Today, people also set off fireworks. However, the purpose of the fireworks is not to defeat the monster. It is to eliminate the bad luck of this year and to bring good luck for the new year.

Finally, the true meaning of the Chinese New Year is to share this day with the whole family. Many people are busy with working. They don't have enough time to spend with their families. However, the Chinese New Year provides people a good chance to share a wonderful time with family members. People often do not have enough time to communicate with their families every day, but they can stay with their families on the last day of the year and wait for the first day of the new year to arrive. People can talk about the happiness or success of this year with family members, or people can talk about the goals and plans for the new year. It is a good time for people to find out what their family members have been doing and what they are thinking. It is a great time to enhance the relationship between family members.

The Chinese New Year is an important holiday for Chinese people. It is also a crucial part of Chinese culture. Although Chinese people have many ways to celebrate this day, the true meaning behind these traditional ways is only one. That is to share a wonderful time with family members.

Tsagaan Sar in Mongolia
MENDJARGAL MUNGUNKHUYAG

TSAGAAN SAR IS ONE OF the traditional Mongolian holidays. Every year in February we celebrate it for about four days. These days are Tsagaan Sar's eve, first, second and third. Tsagaan Sar, which means white moon, is a holiday to celebrate the new year. When February comes, everyone is excited to celebrate "white moon." Before this holiday, we prepare many things. For instance, we go shopping and get groceries and presents. Also, we clean up everything in the house. We buy new clothes or make traditional clothes. Usually older people like to wear special traditional clothes during these days.

On the first day of the holiday, we get up early in the morning. We make special traditional desserts and delicious foods, such as *buuz* and *bansh*. We cook lamb as the main dish. Also, we make *airag*, one of the traditional drinks made with horse milk. Once we greet our loved ones and show our great respect for our elders, we go to church. We pray and wish that the new year will bring all of us happiness.

Tsagaan Sar is a holiday built on respect, especially the respect for older people. So, younger people respect and adore their elders. During these days, we invite each other into our homes. Also, we exchange gifts and enjoy talking and singing together. We like to watch special holiday wrestling and horse racing on the television, too.

Chinese New Year in Indonesia
VICTORIA BUDIMAN

I COME FROM INDONESIA. INDONESIA HAS the fourth largest population in the world. With this big population, we have a variety in our ethnic backgrounds. Take my family as an example. My great-great grandfather came to Indonesia from Fujian, China. He stayed and married a native Indonesian, and that makes my family and me Indonesian Chinese. As Indonesian Chinese, we have a special celebration called Chinese New Year. Chinese New Year is a national holiday in Indonesia.

Chinese New Year is a celebration based on the lunar calendar. I don't know exactly how they calculate the exact day of Chinese New Year from year to year, but usually we celebrate Chinese New Year sometime in February. What I like about the celebration is every child and most single adults receive lucky money in red envelopes. Lucky money is a symbol of good luck in the new coming year.

The other thing that I like is that we wear new clothes. These new clothes should be red because red is a symbol for luck. My mom always bought our new clothes a week before this event. And we also had to have a haircut. This symbolizes throwing away our past bad luck and growing our new luck.

I also look forward to the food for this celebration. Usually on the Chinese New Year's Eve, we gather together to have a family dinner. We have eight different kinds of dishes on the table. These are fish, chicken, pork, vegetables, noodles, buns, soup and pot-stickers. They all symbolize good fortune and luck. We also have to have sweet oranges and other sweet treats after dinner.

Thinking about Chinese New Year now already makes me excited. I really want to celebrate this event with my family back in my country. I miss my mom's cooking and being together for a nice family dinner.

Lunar New Year
HOA NGUYEN

IF CHRISTMAS IS THE BIGGEST holiday in America, Tet, also called the Lunar New Year, is the biggest one in Vietnam. We usually take two weeks off from work and school for this event. Everyone is excited to prepare for the Tet holidays. We clean up and decorate our houses. In the parks, there are flower markets that sell trees and flowers. For Tet, people usually buy peach blossoms with pink flowers and put them in the living room. While the peach tree is preferred in the north, the *hoa mai* plant is commonly used for this ceremony in the south because of the warm weather. Different from the peach blossom, *hoa mai* has yellow petals.

While enjoying the festivities, we don't forget our ancestors. A five-fruit tray that has different kinds of fruit is put on an altar to honor our ancestors. One thing that can't be missed during the Tet holidays is *banh chung*. *Banh chung* is molded into a square shape and wrapped in banana leaves. It is made of rice, pork, and beans. *Banh chung* symbolizes the Earth and the fertile soil of Vietnam.

We spend the first couple of days of Lunar New Year visiting our relatives and neighbors around us. What we do most during these days is visit, eat, and play. Kids also usually get lucky money from adults. The Tet holiday is to celebrate Lunar New Year, but it is also the occasion for families and friends to gather and meet each other. I really enjoy my time during the Tet holiday each year. When I was a kid, I always waited for Tet one month before it came. The reason was to get lucky money and have time to play. Now that I've grown up, I like Tet because of its exciting and warm atmosphere. It is a time to meet everyone in my extended family.

The Excitement of Tet
VY TRAN

PEOPLE ALL KNOW THAT EVERY country has its own culture and some unique holidays. My country is no exception. The Lunar New Year, Tet in Vietnam, is like American Thanksgiving and Christmas. Vietnamese spend a long time preparing and a long time celebrating with their families.

Tet is the specific Vietnamese name used for the New Year holiday. We celebrate Tet at the same time as Chinese New Year, which follows the lunar calendar. The Tet season usually starts between January and March, which is about December to February on the lunar calendar. At this time of the year everyone in Vietnam tries his or her best to get back to the family house and spend time with their relatives. Since people have their own busy life with different schedules for work, normally they cannot spend as much time together as often as they want. So Tet is the best time for people to rest, relax, and most especially be home.

Some people who go to work or school in faraway cities like to take a break and to go back to their hometown. They are eager to get their tickets booked, which helps to make Tet's atmosphere more animated. During this season, people go crazy with shopping. There's a funny but true saying, "Work the whole year, just for ten days of spending." People have to buy different kinds of things. For example, people buy enough food to keep in reserve for the couple of days the grocery stores are closed, and they buy gifts for friends, co-workers, and of course, family. During Tet, students all over the country have at least ten days in a row off. People who go to work or have their own business also take four or five days off. Consequently, people have time to prepare everything before the first day of Tet. After the first day, everyone just wants to stay home, welcome his or her guests, and enjoy the spring season with family.

After shopping, cleaning the house is next. New Year to the Vietnamese starts with everything clean and new. People clean and decorate their house not only because of tradition but also because of their guests' visiting. The Vietnamese really love to hear sweet things and compliments on Tet because they believe that brings good luck. They hope to have those sweet things for the whole year. While cleaning the house, people take special care of the ancestor's altar. To the Vietnamese, New Year is the only time and the best time for their ancestor to come back and spend time with family. Taking care of the altar expresses respect for the returning ancestor.

The first day of Tet is the most important day because it symbolizes all the activities in the whole year. Since people love to have the best first day of the year, they try their best to prepare for it. So Vietnamese want to pay off all of their debts before the New Year begins. They believe that if they resolve everything before the first day, they will have a carefree year. Everything the Vietnamese try to do to prepare for the first day — decorating the house, dressing up with new clothes, preparing enough food for guests — everything has to be perfectly done to welcome in the best new year possible.

There is one unique but really interesting custom. The first visitor on Tet is very important to every Vietnamese family. The first visitor on Tet brings luck to the house. So be careful about going to someone's house on the first day of Tet if you are not invited! The guests know they play an important role for their friend's new year, so they often visit the house with meaningful gifts and their best wishes.

The Vietnamese are supposed to say sweet, good things during Tet. Since people pray for happiness and peace, they must be the ones to begin and keep their first days of the year beautiful. The parents will encourage the kids to set a new goal and promise to reach that goal in the new year. The kids will be dressed up, visit the parents' friends' houses, and get lucky money from the adults. Some of the kids like to keep that money in order to keep luck for the whole year. However, most kids spend their money right away because this time is the perfect time for them to buy whatever they want without asking permission from strict adults.

The Tet holiday is a special occasion to be together. People spend time with family and other loved ones. They enjoy some activities that they haven't had time for during the year. These are the first thoughts in a Vietnamese's mind during Tet season. No matter how busy people are, no matter how far away they live, they go back to where they grew up. Normally people just stay home once they get there, so there is barely anyone on the road. However, if people need to go out to get something done, the deserted atmosphere outside whispers to them to get back to their warm house as soon as possible. There's no place as warm and peaceful as home, right?

The Tet holiday is pretty much just like that. People enjoy the holiday as much as they can. After a few days, everyone goes back to what they are supposed to do for the rest of the year. No matter how long, no matter how many days off people have, it is still not enough. Still, people leave eagerly to start their new routine and wait for another new year, another Tet.

Sol-nal in Korea
YEJIN LEE

KOREA HAS TWO DIFFERENT NEW Year's days, one based on the solar calendar and the other based on the lunar calendar. The more widely preferred one is the lunar New Year's Day, called So-nal. Sol-nal is a day for the whole family to be reunited and for refreshing everyone's common, regular life at the beginning of a year. The day has many special meanings and events.

First, in the morning of Sol-nal, everyone dresses in specially prepared, traditional clothes. Generally, these clothes are decorated with five colors. They are called Sol-bim. Also, everyone in the family gathers at their eldest male relative's home to perform *Cha-rye*, ancestral memorial rites.

Second, we eat special food called *Ttok-kuk*. This is a soup with slices of white rice cake boiled in a thick beef broth topped with bright garnishes. This food means "adding age." So, people believe if they have a bowl of this soup, they become one year older. Koreans traditionally add one to their age, not after their birthdays, but at the New Year.

Third, after the big, very special breakfast, the younger people bow to their elders, wishing them health and long life, good luck, and prosperity throughout the whole year. This bowing is called Se-bae or Jol. Often, kids prepare small, beautifully decorated purses to hold the money that the elders give them after the bowing. And, after the long bowing period, youngsters go outside to fly kites, spin tops (for boys) and enjoy Korean seesaw games (for girls). Also, inside, people play Yut-no-ri, a game played with four wooden sticks and checkers.

In conclusion, Korean people eat, talk, and play all day long and enjoy their large family reunion from great-grandparents to great-grandchildren. It is the most important Korean holiday.

CHAPTER THREE
Full Moon Festivals

My Mid-Autumn Festival Tradition
Mid-Autumn Festival in China
Being Together
Lantern Festival in Taiwan
Chuseok With My Husband's Family
Cambodia's Water Festival
Loy Krathong

Full Moon Festivals

My Mid-Autumn Festival Tradition
SARAH NIELSEN

I WAS NOT BORN IN CHINA, and I do not have any Chinese ancestors. But I have celebrated the Chinese Mid-Autumn Festival since 1988. Mid-Autumn Festival is one of my favorite holidays. It is a time for me to remember and feel connected to friends and family who live far away from me.

In the fall of 1988, I moved to Beijing, the capital of China, to be an English teacher in a university. I was 23 years old, and I was very excited to have my first teaching job. I was excited to be living in a new country and to be learning a new language. In fact, every day was an exciting adventure for me. But, as you know, moving to a new country can also sometimes make you feel homesick and lonely and confused.

In those early days in Beijing, I did miss my family and friends and everything that was familiar to me. One evening, some of the English students came to the foreign teacher dormitory where I was living. They knocked on my door and the doors of the other foreign teachers. The students asked us, "Do you know what today is?" We foreign teachers looked at each other and shook our heads no. We didn't know that it was a special day.

The students said that they would tell us all about the special day and invited us to go up on the roof of the dormitory building. All of the foreign teachers were curious about the special day and happy to have this surprise visit from our students. We followed the students up the stairs and out the door onto the roof. Right away I knew the special day had something to do with the moon. I had never seen such a big, beautiful moon rising. Time stopped for a moment. There was nothing in the world but me and the shimmering, round moon. The moon seemed to be as bright as the sun, and the night seemed as light as the day.

The students spread out blankets for all of us to sit down on and began to tell the foreign teachers the story of Mid-Autumn Festival. They explained that two lovers were separated on the day of Mid-Autumn Festival thousands of years ago. These two lovers could only meet one day every year during the Mid-Autumn Festival when the moon was at its fullest for the year. The Mid-Autumn Festival, the students said, was a time to be with family. Even if the family could not be together in person, on Mid-Autumn Festival the family members could feel connected to each other by looking at the full moon.

We were all silent after the story was finished. The students were far away from their families. The foreign teachers were far away from their families, too. But as we looked at the full moon rising, we could all feel our family members right next to us.

After some quiet time together, one of the students took out some round cakes and some brandy. The student explained that the round cakes were called moon cakes, the traditional food for Mid-Autumn Festival. We ate our moon cakes filled with lotus seed paste and a single salted egg yolk. We sipped some brandy. We watched that beautiful moon rise and rise. We were quiet, and we were noisy. We talked about our families. We laughed and joked with each other. We sat silently, thinking about our happy times at home and the happy time shared with new friends.

Many years have passed since I first celebrated Mid-Autumn Festival with my students in Beijing. I now live in the United States, but I still celebrate Mid-Autumn Festival every year. Before the festival, I visit a Chinese bakery in my city and buy some moon cakes. On the night of the festival, I share a moon cake with my husband, and we wait for the moon to rise. I watch the full moon light up the night, and I think about all the people I love who are far away from me. For a few moments, we are all together, connected through that beautiful autumn full moon.

Mid-Autumn Festival in China
PINGFAN HE

THE MID-AUTUMN FESTIVAL IS THE second biggest festival in China. Only the Chinese New Year is bigger. In the evening of the fifteenth day of the eighth lunar month of the Chinese calendar, traditional Chinese family members will get together at their parents' home and eat a big dinner. After that, they will sit under the full moon, drink tea or wine, eat moon cakes, and enjoy the glorious full moon. On this night you will miss even more those family members who cannot come back because this day's moon is especially bright, especially circular, and especially big.

There are a lot of interesting legends about the Mid-Autumn Festival. The tale of Chang Er flying to the moon is my favorite.

A long time ago there were ten suns in the sky. It was very hot. People could not live. At that time there was a very strong man named Yi. He shot down nine suns with a bow and arrow. The last sun was frightened. It admitted it was wrong and promised to get up early and work until late evening every day for the people on Earth. From that time onward, Yi became a famous person. Later, he married a very beautiful and kindhearted girl named Chang Er. Their lives were very happy and full of love. Yi often hunted a lot of animals and Chang Er would give those animals to the villagers. One day, Yi got a small bag of magical pills from a Taoist. The Taoist gave these pills to Yi because Yi did a lot of good things for people. If Yi ate half of the pills, he would never die. If he ate all of them, he would become celestial and would fly to heaven. Yi returned to his home and passed these pills to his wife. He wanted his wife to keep these pills so they could share them later at some good time. Then they would live together forever.

Yi had many students who were learning how to hunt from him. Feng Meng was one of his students, but he was a bad person. He wanted to steal the pills from Yi. On the fifteenth day of the eighth month of the Chinese lunar calendar, Yi went out to hunt. Feng Meng pretended that he was ill, and he entered Chang Er's home and tried to force her to give him the pills. Chang Er didn't want to give them to him. She called for help, but nobody was around.

Finally, she swallowed all of the pills. Suddenly, she felt like a swallow and started to fly slowly. She passed through a window and flew up to the sky. She didn't want to abandon her husband and her home, so she flew to the moon because it is nearest to the earth.

Yi came home and wanted to get his wife back, but it was too late. He could just see his wife's shadow on the moon. That night, the moon was very bright and circular. Yi was very sad. The villagers said Chang Er would come back. They asked Yi to wait for Chang Er one year later on the fifteenth day of the eighth lunar month. Yi missed his wife, so he planted a lot of fruit trees in their garden because Change Er liked the garden. He made moon cakes to symbolize reunion. He wanted his wife to come back and to live with him together again. But year after year, his wife did not come back.

Gradually, people created the Mid-Autumn Festival. They prepare moon cakes and fruits. Family members return home and eat dinner together. Then they eat moon cakes and fruit symbolizing reunion. Today this festival is for celebrating the harvest of the autumn. I like the Mid-Autumn Festival because I love all family members eating together. I like moon cakes, and I especially appreciate the love story.

Being Together
YU JIE LIU

During the daytime, mid-autumn festival seems like a regular day. People go about their regular business, going to school or work. The festival is a celebration of the moon, so the Mid-Autumn Festival itself is held at night. The mothers of the family will set up a table and prepare a lot of food to place on the table.

Different types of fruits and nuts play an important role in the festival because it occurs during the harvest period. Even more important are moon cakes, a food unique to the holiday. This food is a symbol for the moon. Moon cakes are a favorite of every age, from young children to grandparents. Moon cakes are usually made of lotus seed butter with a salted duck egg in the middle, but there can be other fillings inside the cakes as well.

Usually on the night of Mid-Autumn Festival, all the family members should be present and sit around the table to have dinner together. This time is called *tuan yuan*, which means "being together." There is a special dessert prepared for after dinner called *tang yuan*. Eating *tang yuan* is a kind of celebration of all the family members being together. Eating *tang yuan* symbolizes the wish for family members to be safe out in the world. It also symbolizes the hope for family members to sit around the table and eat the *tang yuan* together again next year.

When everything is prepared, the family waits for the moon to rise.

The tables are set outdoors so that the family members are able to get the perfect view of the moon rising. After the moon has risen, the dinner can begin, and family members can enjoy the moonlight. Most of the time, the children eat as fast as possible because they want to go out to the street with their lanterns to walk and play. In some cities, people also light fireworks, and the sky is decorated not only with the moon and stars, but also with the beautiful fireworks.

Chinese people celebrate the moon because the shape of the moon is round. The word for round in Chinese is *yuan*. *Yuan* also means perfect, so the moon symbolizes the perfect family where no one is lost or far away. Mid-Autumn Festival is a very important day to Chinese people. It shows how family is important to every Chinese person.

Lantern Festival in Taiwan
ANGELA HIRSCH

THE LANTERN FESTIVAL, WHICH IS also known as the Shang Yuan Festival, takes place on the fifteenth day of the first moon. This festival is the last in a series of springtime celebrations after the Lunar New Year. The Lantern Festival, considered a second New Year, is widely celebrated by families all around Taiwan.

On the night of the festival, decorative lanterns are everywhere. Children carry the lanterns to decorate temples. The most beautiful lanterns are made in the shapes of birds, beasts, and historical figures. In fact, every year all over Taiwan during the Lantern Festival, we have competitions to highlight these glowing works of art. The largest and most famous of these lantern competitions is held annually in the capitol city of Taipei at Chiang Kai-shek Memorial Hall Plaza. Thousands of lantern watchers attend the Taipei

Lantern Festival competition. Recently an interesting new tradition was added as part of the Lantern Festival. The lantern puzzle parties are now held on this night.

The night sky during the Lantern Festival is illuminated not only by lanterns, but also by the Tainan Yanshui fireworks display and Taipei Pinghsi Sky Lanterns, which are known together as fireworks in the southern sky and lanterns in the northern sky. Many other regional folk activities for the Lantern Festival also include firework displays.

In addition to the displays of fireworks and lanterns, the Lantern Festival is also celebrated by eating a special food, called *tan yuan*. Eating *tan yuan* is an important custom that symbolizes family union and is an essential part of the day's festivities.

The various Lantern Festival customs provide people with rich entertainment. For example, the lantern displays of historical figures and the lantern puzzle parties are wonderful to experience. But the lantern customs also educate people through their expression of ancient wisdom. In addition, the variety of magnificent lanterns shows different folk art techniques. This art impresses me deeply in both my heart and mind.

Chuseok with My Husband's Family

SUSON LEE

CHUSEOK IS CELEBRATED ON THE fifteenth day of the eighth lunar month. We go to visit our ancestral graves and honor or respect our ancestors. I liked this holiday more before I got married because married women have many things to do.

My husband and I used to go to Andong, where my husband's parents lived, to spend Chuseok together with family and relatives. Normally it takes five hours to get to Andong from the place I lived. Everybody, however, goes back to their hometown for Chuseok, so the traffic is very terrible every year. It took twelve hours to get to my husband's house. Even though I was tired, I couldn't resist going.

I had to wake up early to prepare everything because I am the daughter-in-law. Also my husband's father is the oldest of his brothers, so his brothers and their children got together in my husband's father's house every Chuseok. There were about twenty people. They stayed overnight to have Chuseok the next day. Can you imagine?

My husband's parents were strict. They regarded the ceremony as important. We made special offerings which are *songpyeon*, rice cake, fresh seasoned vegetables, and the first products of the year for the ceremony. Later, we visited our ancestral graves and performed low bows twice to each ancestor. We cleaned the graves and made ancestor memorial services. After the ceremony was finished, I could go in my parent's house. It is a Korean rule.

When I came to America, I felt the culture of America is very different from my country. For example, they prepare simple food potluck style and share their joy together by talking then eating. Also, according to Korean customs, men don't do kitchen work, only women work on holidays. I think it is unfair.

During the holiday, my children had a good time. Most of the time, they didn't have an opportunity to meet their relatives. We enjoyed playing Korean traditional games together. Also my husband's parents were very happy that they had time with many relatives. As our parents were getting older, they missed seeing their children and grandchildren.

When I am older, I will want to enjoy Chuseok with my grandchildren. In spite of the hard work, if I go back to Korea someday, I will try more convincingly to enjoy the holiday.

Cambodia's Water Festival
VANESSA MASSEN

EACH YEAR IN CAMBODIA, THERE are many holidays to celebrate. They all have their own meaning and reason. One of my favorite holidays is called Water Festival. We usually celebrate it at the end of October or the beginning of November. It depends on the full moon. The holiday is to wish and pray for all the farmers in the whole country and to celebrate the changing flow of the Tonle Sap River back to the Mekong River. This is a very unique river in the world. It is the only river to change the flow of the current twice each year. At the Water Festival the river returns to the normal downstream flow. This ancient festival includes a ceremony with seeds, boat racing, and fireworks.

People do not need to prepare much before this holiday, but many people like to buy new clothes for going out on the holiday. On the first morning of the three-day Water Festival, the King of Cambodia goes to a national traditional palace. This palace is only used for this holiday. The prime minister and all the people working for the government must be there also. To begin, a girl from the palace will prepare six kinds of grains. There are red beans, green beans, black-eyed beans, sticky rice seeds, rice seeds, corn seeds, and one bowl of water. After the six kinds of grains are prepared, people will bring a big white cow to eat the seeds. They cannot force the cow to eat. If the cow eats lots of rice, it means that the rice plants will be good for the whole season. If the cow eats other seeds or grains, it means the same good fortune for those seeds or grains. They take the cow to eat the seeds because most of the farmers in Cambodia use cows to work their fields. After the cow has eaten, the king will pray. The morning ceremony usually takes about two hours.

In the afternoon, we have one more ceremony that is called boat racing. The farmers in each village get a chance to race their boats in competition with other villages. They have their own decorated boats and uniforms in different styles and colors. This makes the Mekong River in the capital, Phnom Penh, look colorful. The villagers race with each other until there are only three groups left. Then they will be the first, second, and third place winners for the whole year. They race the decorated boats in order to please the god of the water. Their wish is to please the god and to ask for the right amount of rain, not too much and not too little. The farmers need water for their crops.

At night, people continue to celebrate. Many young people usually go out because there is an extremely big concert at the central park in Phnom Penh. There is also another ceremony at the river. The ministries of the government make their own floats, called *brotips*. These floats are decorated with beautiful colors and lights that are so bright. They flow along the river and make the river look beautiful. Finally, people light fireworks at midnight. I usually stand on the highest balcony of my house with my sister and wait for the fireworks. I always feel happy on the Water Festival holiday because I love to see the beautiful fireworks. I love this holiday.

Loy Krathong
SOMTHAWIN KROGH

ON THE NIGHT OF THE full moon of the twelfth lunar month, the tide in the rivers is at its highest, and the moon is at its brightest, creating a romantic setting ideal for lovers. The Thai people choose this day to hold the Loy Krathong Festival, or the Festival of Light. Loy Krathong is one of the two most recognized festivals in the country. This fall festival dates back more than seven hundred years. The name, Loy Krathong, means to float a lotus shaped vessel, and this is what people do.

Every year I celebrate Loy Krathong with my family. Early in the day, my family and I go to the temple to pray. Then we go back home, and we have lunch together. After lunch, my father and my brother cut a part of the banana tree to make our lotus shaped *krathong*. The *krathong* is made of banana leaves, or the layers of the trunk of the banana tree, or a spider lily plant, so it will float and hold special items. People put flowers, three sticks of incense, some coins, and a candle on the lotus shaped float. The *krathongs* are much more creative these days as many more materials are available.

When we finish making the *krathong*, we go to watch the parade downtown. The parade always has large decorated *krathongs*. They are always beautiful, so we enjoy it very much. In the evening after dinner, my family and I go to the river for the Loy Krathong celebration. Thousands of people go to the canals and rivers with their *krathongs* for the Festival of Light. First, they light the candle and put some coins in the *krathong*. Then they silently make a wish and carefully place their *krathong* in the water and release it into the current of the river or canal. They watch intently as the flow of water sends each *krathong* silently downstream, hoping that the candle on their floating *krathong* will not go out. The flame is said to signify longevity, fulfillment of wishes, and release from sins. A couple who makes a wish together on Loy Krathong is thought to stay together in the future.

Once all the *krathongs* are out of sight, families return home. Everyone is tired and ready to go to bed. I miss Loy Krathong in Thailand, and I also miss my family very much.

CHAPTER FOUR
Honoring Special People

Federal Holidays Honoring People
Indian's Day in Peru
Hina Matsuri in Japan
Children's Day in Japan
Shichi-Go-San
Thank You, Teachers in Korea
A Holiday in My Native Country, China
The Dragon Boat Festival
Mother's Day in Colombia

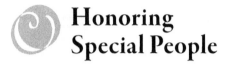

Honoring Special People

Federal Holidays Honoring People

MARILYN MARQUIS

*I*N THE UNITED STATES, WE have some federal holidays to honor people for a variety of reasons. These people contributed something significant to the formation or improvement of the nation. The federal holidays in the United States are generally the same as the state holidays, but we do not have any national holidays. On federal holidays, the post office is closed and so are many banks. That is how you will know if the holiday is a federal holiday. We have federal, state, and local holidays, and businesses and schools can decide which holidays to celebrate. For example, sometimes the college is open, but the public elementary schools are closed. This sometimes confuses people. Most federal holidays are now Monday holidays. This tradition began in the 1970s. The dates change each year, but the holidays are always on a particular Monday. This makes three-day weekends for workers and students.

The first Monday holiday of the year is on the third Monday in January. This is Martin Luther King, Jr. Day. We honor him for drawing attention to segregation and the unequal treatment of African Americans. He organized peaceful protests and civil disobedience to change laws and protect the rights of everyone. He helped everyone, black and white, find the courage to ask for freedom.

On the third Monday of February, we honor special presidents. We honor President Abraham Lincoln and President George Washington. They were both born in February, and they were both very important in American history. The next Monday holiday that celebrates people is the first Monday in September. This is Labor Day in the United States. We honor the workers who have helped to build the economic strength of this country. In October, we honor Christopher Columbus on the second Monday. Columbus is honored in many countries in the Americas because he was the first European to visit this continent.

Another important holiday honoring people is Veterans Day, November Eleventh. This holiday honors all those who have served this country as members of the Army, the Navy, the Marines, and the Air Force. On this day, many people display the American flag on their homes or businesses. This is also the day when the president goes to Arlington National Cemetery to place a wreath at the Tomb of the Unknowns. Many people go to the cemetery to visit the graves of loved ones who died in a war.

For these federal holidays we honor special people, but we do not have any national traditions. We do not have festivals in our cities or towns. There is no special food.

Sometimes people just appreciate having a day off of work or school; they do not always think about the reason for the holiday.

Indian's Day in Peru
SAIDA ALVARADO

IN PERU, WE CELEBRATE INDIAN'S Day on June 24 every year. This is an ancient holiday, since the time of the Inca civilization. I really like this holiday because it reminds us of the legacy of a great culture, their good customs, and their wisdom. It is an historical holiday, and we celebrate it with family and friends. People throughout Peru celebrate this holiday, but the biggest celebration place is Cuzco. Many people go there from different cities in Peru, and many tourists from all around the world go as well.

This holiday is a colorful party and requires a great deal of preparation. People begin by preparing their traditional Inca clothes for the parade. These clothes are bright and colorful with many decorations and jewelry. People also prepare traditional foods on special ceramic dishes. The traditional food is made from grains like lima beans, purple corn, white corn, and wheat, among others. People use these grains to prepare soups, stews, and desserts. A special drink of the Incas is *chichi de jors*. It is made from grains and fermented under the ground for a long time.

The families go to parades where people re-enact the Inca's customs, teachings, and traditions. We enjoy having fun with relatives and friends. Every family prepares and shares food. One of the Inca's teachings was to do cooperative work by sharing and learning together. My grandmother enjoys cooking with people. They prepare dessert, *mazamora morada*, with purple corn and different fruits.

I think that it is the most beautiful holiday. We have the clothes, food, and decorations to remind us about the goodness of our native people who continue suffering when we ignore them.

Hina Matsuri in Japan
TERUMI WALDMAN

MOST COUNTRIES CELEBRATE TRADITIONAL EVENTS. In Japan, Hina Matsuri, or doll festival, takes place on March 3, the third day of the third month. On this day we celebrate Girls' Day. Starting mid-to-late February, families with daughters display traditional dolls. The dolls symbolize their hope for their daughters to grow up healthy and happy. Traditionally, many parents or grandparents begin their first display for their daughter, called Hatsu Zekku, when she is just a year old. Most displays consist of a prince and a princess. The dolls wear old traditional *kimonos* like those of the Japanese imperial family. Elaborate displays include the dolls in a five-tier or seven-tier display case. The display includes courtiers, candy, diamond shaped rice cakes, peach blossoms, toys, and tiny furniture.

One superstition associated with this holiday says if someone puts the dolls away too late after the holiday, the daughter will never marry. In modern times because of more gender neutral celebrations, many people do not celebrate this holiday now. Hina Matsuri, however, is still a brilliant day for girls.

Children's Day in Japan
YUKIKO TAKASHIMA

WE HAVE FOURTEEN NATIONAL HOLIDAYS every year in Japan. New Year's Day is probably the most important. However, I like another holiday best. It is Children's Day and Golden Week. We celebrate Children's Day on May 5, the fifth day of the fifth month. There are several reasons I like this holiday.

First of all, everyone has a week-long vacation during Golden Week. On April 29, we start the celebrations with the emperor's birthday. Then we celebrate Constitution Day, and finally, on May 5, we celebrate Children's Day. Usually we take a long vacation together over the long holiday. When I worked in Japan, I often went to a foreign country for one week. I enjoyed holidays in Hawai-i and Thailand.

Second, the school had special programs when I was a student. Many parents stayed home from work to join the school programs. I liked having my father come and study with me. For example, we made an airplane with papers, or we ran together in the gymnasium. It was a wonderful experience.

There is also some special food on this day. For example, everyone eats special rice cakes called *kashiwamochi*. These have delicious red bean paste inside. Families with young boys hang a flag with a picture of a carp outside their house.

Shichi-Go-San
YUKIKO EGAWA

IF YOU VISIT JAPAN IN the middle of November, you might see many young children at shrines, wearing beautifully crafted *kimonos*. They are celebrating Shichi-Go-San. This is a traditional Japanese ceremony for children of the ages of seven, five, and three. The name of the holiday translates to seven-five-three in Japanese. Families go to a shrine to pray for a healthy life for their children. Originally, Shichi-Go-San was celebrated on November 15, but now many people celebrate it on one of the weekends either before or after the traditional date. Children wear a traditional *kimono* or formal dress and eat *chitose-ame*. Parents take a lot of pictures of their children as family keepsakes.

Children are fascinated by the *kimono*. This traditional Japanese clothing is unusual for them. They wear the traditional clothes at the age of three to symbolize the end of their infancy and the beginning of early childhood. We celebrate Shichi-Go-San for both boys and girls. After that, we celebrate the age of five for boys and seven for girls. After the age of three, many girls will grow their hair long to have a nice *kimono* hairstyle for their seven-year-old celebration. The age of five is the special occasion for boys to wear a traditional *kimono* with a *haori* jacket and *hakama* trousers, just like the Japanese samurai warriors of old. In addition, they proudly carry a toy sword, *katana*.

For seven-year-old girls, Shichi-Go-San is a really special day. They wear very beautiful *kimonos* and makeup on their faces. Their hairstyle is in a special way with *kanzashi*, special hair ornaments. Also, they carry cute handbags made of *kimono* cloth, and they wear *zouri*, Japanese sandals. These girls look very beautiful, like a bride or princess in an old Japanese castle. They are proud of themselves, and they walk like real princesses. When I was three years old, my grandmother made my *kimono*. She was a professional *kimono* maker. I could wear the same one for my seven-year-old celebration because *kimonos* can be adjusted for growth.

Chitose-ame is another important symbol of Shichi-Go-San. It means "thousand year's candy" in Japanese. Children will eat this special candy to have a long and healthy life. This unusually long candy is the symbol of long life, and it can only be purchased in November for Shichi-Go-San. There are a few pieces in a bag, and each candy is colored either red or white, which are lucky colors. The bag is also specially designed for this celebration. It has pictures of a crane and turtle. These illustrations recall a famous Japanese saying, "The crane lives a thousand years, and the turtle lives ten thousand years." These creatures are symbols of long life. I still remember eating that candy after my celebration. It didn't taste very sweet like western candies, but I liked it.

The photographs of the children are special for us Japanese. At my three year-old celebration, my picture was taken by a professional photographer. I had short hair with a big ribbon on my head. Recently, I showed it to my two sons. I thought I looked like a doll in my picture; however, my kids said I looked like a boy. Although we've been living in the United States for several years, I have my younger son's Shichi-Go-San picture. When he was five years old, we went back to Tokyo for summer vacation. We rented a beautiful boy's *kimono* with *haori* and *hakama*, and we asked a photographer to take his picture. Even without a *katana*, he was very happy to be a little *samurai*.

Shichi-Go-San is an important day for the Japanese.

Parents pray that their children have a long healthy life, and children experience Japanese tradition through wearing a *kimono* and tasting *chitose-ame*.

Thank You, Teachers in Korea
KYUNG-JIN KIM

THE WAYS OF CELEBRATING HOLIDAYS can be different all around the world. For instance, people may wear traditional costumes or eat different foods depending on where they live and what they believe. Yet, every country or ethnicity celebrates similar kinds of holidays, such as New Year's Day, National Foundation Day, or Independence Day. Korea also has some special holidays. I would like to introduce Teachers' Day.

Teachers' Day is May 15 every year. Students express their appreciation to their teachers on this day. Some schools close on Teachers' Day, but a number of schools in Korea hold a special class. First of all, students, especially those beyond junior high, prepare an early morning surprise party for the teacher. There is a party in each classroom. Students decorate the classroom with balloons and write some messages on the blackboard. Also, they prepare some songs for the teacher. Then, they gather some presents in front of the classroom and wait for the teacher. After the teacher comes into the classroom, they spend enjoyable time. This is the important part of the day, I think. During the party, the students show things they prepared for their teacher. A student leader is likely to read a letter or give a bunch of flowers to the teacher. Students and the teacher talk together, drink delicious beverages, and share some cake. All of them enjoy this time. After the party, some parents or celebrities are likely to come to the school and address students about valuable lessons. Also, some college students who graduated from the high school visit their former teachers.

When I was a freshman in high school, my class gave a couple of small turtles to our teacher as a present. Because the turtles have a very long life, they symbolize our hope that the teacher will remember us as long as the turtles live.

After the events, the teacher's room is filled with a lot of presents and flowers. Consequently, some teachers feel uncomfortable getting very expensive gifts. So those teachers prefer to close school on Teachers' Day.

In conclusion, the real meaning of the day is that students express how much they appreciate their teacher. The teachers receive students' thankful hearts. Thus, this day is meaningful both for the teachers and the students.

A Holiday in My Native Country, China
BERNARD CHANG

DUAN WU, OR DRAGON BOAT, Festival is held on the fifth day of the fifth month of the lunar calendar in China. I always looked forward to the Duan Wu Festival in China. Although it is not an official national holiday, it is still widely celebrated especially by people in southern China.

When I was in China on this day, I used to enjoy watching dragon boat races and eating *zhong zhi*. These are sweet rice, meat, preserved fruits and sugar wrapped in bamboo leaves and tied with colored thread. Families used to make most of their food because eating out or buying ready-to-eat food was expensive. Usually, a week before the festival, my grandmother began to shop for the ingredients for making the *zhong zhi*. On the day before Duan Wu Festival, my female cousins helped my grandmother wrap *zhong zhi*. On the day of the festival, while my grandmother was boiling the *zhong zhi*, my cousins and I would go to the river bank to watch dragon boat races. While watching races, I used to see some people also throw *zhong zhi* into the river. I thought that it was a big waste of food.

In middle school, I learned the significance of people throwing *zhong zhi* into the river to feed fish. The *zhong zhi* were for the fish, so the fish would not eat Qu Yuan. Qu Yuan was a great poet of the State of Chin, one of seven states in China many years ago. The state of Chin, in the north, started to unite China by military force about 2,300 years ago. The Chin used military force to unite China. Qu Yuan drowned himself on the fifth day of the fifth month in protest of the emperor. He thought the emperor should not give in to the aggression of the state of Chin. Qu Yuan's patriotism deeply touched the people of the State of Chun. When people learned of Qu Yuan's drowning they began to throw rice wrapped in bamboo leaves into the river to feed the fish. They hoped that the fish would not have to eat Qu Yuan. At the same time, many people took their boats to find Qu Yuan. His body was never found. Later, in remembrance of Qu Yuan, people began the custom in south China of having dragon boat races and eating *zhong zhi* on the fifth day of the fifth month.

The Dragon Boat Festival

YANG XING GONG

The dragon boat festival, also known as the Double Fifth Festival, occurs on the fifth day of the fifth moon of the lunar calendar. It is one of the three most important annual Chinese festivals. The other two are the Autumn Moon Festival and the Chinese New Year.

This summer festival concerns a famous Chinese scholar-statesman named Qu Yuan. Three hundred years before the birth of Christ is called the Warring States Period in China. Qu Yuan enjoyed the full confidence and respect of the emperor, but eventually that changed. Qu Yuan could not regain the emperor's favor, so, on the fifth day of the fifth moon in the year 295 BC he drowned himself in the Milo River.

The people respected this honest man so they jumped into their boats and rushed out in a vain search for him. This is the Dragon Boat Festival's history.

Another activity of the Festival is the making and eating of a kind of dumpling called *zhong zhi*. People throw cooked rice into the water as a sacrifice to their dead hero. They wrap the rice in bamboo leaves, and stuff them with ham, egg yokes, sausage, and nuts. Today we still eat *zhong zhi* and watch the boat races.

Mother's Day in Colombia

MARIELA ALFARO

Mother's day in colombia is a very special and important day. People want to show their respect and appreciation on this day. In Colombia, mothers are very hard workers. Mothers often work at their jobs all day and also care for their children when they finish a day at work. Many Colombian mothers have their own businesses in their homes, so they can take care of their children and work at the same time. Some work in legal professions and business professions, and others work in restaurants or do domestic work. Regardless of their professions, Colombian mothers are conservative in their customs and are very strict with disciplining children. They try to raise the children with a close family relationship and do not tolerate misbehavior or bad manners. Women continue to care for their children even after those children marry and have children of their own. For these reasons, Colombian mothers are considered the principal member in the family.

Mothers in Colombia want their entire family to gather for a celebration on Mother's Day, so they arrange the celebration. The celebration might be at home or in a restaurant, but the important point is to eat together. The family usually prepares gifts for the mother. They may bring flowers, clothes, or jewelry. Some may make handicrafts for mothers. Others clean her house and cook for her.

The government and private companies also hold special events for Mother's Day. There are usually public and company concerts and theater performances with singing and dramas. At church there is a special mass. The schools also celebrate Mother's Day with music, poetry, and dance. All of these events teach children to respect and love their mothers.

CHAPTER FIVE
Remembering Ancestors

A Unique Chinese Holiday, Ching Ming
Tomb Sweeping Day
The Korean Death Ceremony
Obon: When Spirits Return
Pchum Ben Festival
Days of the Dead
Day of the Dead in Mexico
Dia de Los Muertos

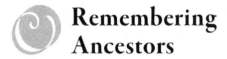
Remembering Ancestors

A Unique Chinese Holiday, Ching Ming
KEUNG LAM

*I*N THE UNITED STATES, PEOPLE celebrate many Chinese holidays. However, they do not have one that was most important in the ancient times, Ching Ming. Ching Ming is a holiday in my native country, China. On this holiday, people go to their ancestors' graves to show their respect and give them things to enjoy. Descendants show respect for their ancestors and recall their contributions. I notice that the many American-born Chinese do not know about this traditional Chinese holiday.

On Ching Ming holiday, people take many things like cooked chicken, fried pork, and fruit to their ancestors' grave for their ancestors' spirit to enjoy. Sometimes it may be a hundred miles of travel and involve a great deal of difficulty. Many people in China do not drive like people in the United States. Even elderly descendants will use their hands, arms, and shoulders to carry heavy loads. They drag goods along the road or take them on the train or bus. They try to arrive at their ancestors' grave at the perfect time. They obey the rules as set forth from their parents because the procedure is very serious. The traditions for this holiday are passed down through each generation.

On that day, usually in early April, people do not need to dress well. Everybody wears casual clothes because at the grave, the family builds a small fire. They burn special paper money which is used only for that day. Some people use sticks and paper to build a house, horse, woman, or anything they imagine their ancestor would like. They burn the offerings in front of the grave. They believe these things will go to their dead ancestors. This holiday is unique for Chinese. I have never seen the same customs in another country.

As the second son in a traditional Chinese family, I am not responsible for the events of this holiday. It is always the first son's responsibility because in ancient times, the first son inherits all the authority, property, and wealth from the parent. Every year on the Chinese farming calendar, the 18th day of the second month, about the beginning of April on the western calendar, my older brother and his spouse prepare the gifts and travel more than a hundred miles to deliver these gifts to our ancestors.

I don't know how long this traditional ritual can last, but I hope it can last forever. The coming generation needs to be reminded of things their parents and their ancestors did for them. It is the ancestors' efforts and contributions that make life easier.

Tomb Sweeping Day
PIN C. LIU

My country, Taiwan, is blessed with a long history, and its people honor filial piety. It is important to obey our parents and honor our ancestors. We honor our ancestors in our homes all year by cooking their favorite foods and burning paper money for them. We also honor them on a special day, April 5, Tomb Sweeping Day.

On this day we go the cemetery. Since most cemeteries are located in the hills on the outskirts of town, we always bring a shovel to root out the dried grass and plants. Sometimes it takes several hours to clean the graves of all of our ancestors. This time of year it is usually very hot, so cleaning the tombs is especially difficult. We also bring special food to honor the deceased. This might be everyday food like chicken, vegetables, or fish. We light incense sticks and offer a silent tribute to the deceased.

This is also a day when family members are together. When the grave is clean and we finish the ceremony, we often have a family outing. We go to a restaurant and have time together. The most important part of the day is to show respect toward our ancestors on Tomb Sweeping Day.

The Korean Death Ceremony
YUN SUSIE

KOREA HAS A VERY OLD culture and many cultural traditions. Koreans value life and death and cherish their relatives. One of these traditions is a ceremony called Jaesa. It is an ancestor respect ceremony. People give respect to their ancestors by offering a variety of foods and wine. When I lived in Korea, my parents held this ceremony at least twice a year. My mother spent two or three days cooking and preparing for the ceremony. My brother, sister, and I always helped to clean the house. We then placed a very large table in the living room for the special food, fruits, and alcohol for our ancestors.

At the beginning of the ceremony, we recalled the names of our ancestors from a list. My father bowed and offered wine to our oldest ancestors first. In earlier time, only men participated in this ceremony, and the family traced its history from one generation to the next through the son. In my family, my father encouraged every member of the family to participate in Jaesa. My brother, sister, and I all bowed to our ancestors. He is the eldest in his family and still holds this ceremony in honor of his ancestors.

The table is the central place of the ceremony. The food is placed on the table in a special order. Fish is placed on one side of the table, and meat is on the opposite side. Rice is placed near the fish, and a bowl of broth is placed at one end of the table. Next, grilled vegetables are placed on the table. Then *kim chi*, spiced sliced meat, nuts, and fruits are put on the table last. After all of the food is on the table, everyone bows twice, and then my father eats a piece of meat and drinks some wine. At the end of the ceremony, my father burns the list of names of our ancestors. Then my family eats together and offers each other best wishes.

Today in Korea many traditions are no longer practiced. Some people think they are old fashioned. I believe that these traditions are an important part of my inheritance. I appreciate the Korean way of honoring the dead.

Obon: When Spirits Return
KYOKO URAMATSU

ONE OF THE BIGGEST CULTURAL events in Japan is Obon. Obon is a Japanese Buddhist holiday to honor the spirits of our ancestors. Every year on this day, we welcome the spirits of our ancestors to our home. Japanese people believe that the spirits of our ancestors stay at our home for four days from August Thirteenth to August Sixteenth. We hope that they enjoy the time they stay with us.

August 13 is the first day of Obon. On this day we prepare a small fire in the front of the door to let spirits know where the entrance is, so they can come in. We prepare a special meal to honor the spirits. We set an extra place at the table so the spirits can eat with us. In my family, my grandmother cooks something that they used to like, such as *miso* soup, *tempura*, and special rice balls called *onigiri*. She also serves a large glass of *sake*, special Japanese wine.

Obon is also a time for the community to get together. During the four days, we have a huge festival in the center of town. I always love to go to that festival because there are a lot of stands selling traditional foods. I always love to go to the festival wearing traditional Japanese costumes called *yukata*. The most important part of the festival is the dancing. We believe that spirits enjoy dancing with us and this special dance is for celebrating their lives.

There are many reasons why the Obon festival is unique to Japanese culture. We welcome our ancestors back into our homes. We also prepare special meals, with traditional foods. Lastly, we wear the traditional Japanese costume. Doing these things every year keeps Japanese people connected with our culture.

Pchum Ben Festival
ANONYMOUS

Although there are a lot of holidays in Cambodia, the most important holiday for me is Pchum Ben Festival, Feeding Ancestors. It is an annual traditional festival when all Cambodians join in celebrating our culture. This holiday lasts for fifteen days, and it always falls in late September. I really enjoy this holiday because it is a good opportunity for me to dress in traditional clothes, offer food to other spirits, and show respect to my ancestors.

Pchum Ben is the best time of the year to wear traditional dresses. I like this type of dress because it is very colorful and delicate. I can wear *sompot hol* or *sompot phamoung,* silk skirts for Cambodian ladies, in my favorite colors. In fact, I can wear this delicate colorful skirt with a white short sleeve or white long sleeve blouse, *aov pak sor.* Then I add a tiny silk scarf in a color matching the color of the skirt. Finally, if I want to be more traditional, I can clip the scarf with a pin.

This holiday is the best chance for us to offer food to other spirits because some spirits have no living relatives. One day prior to the celebration day, my family and I always buy some ingredients for making steamed sticky rice for the next morning. At 4 o'clock in the morning of the celebration day, my family and I often go to the local temple with the steamed sticky rice. After we arrive at the temple, we go to the Vihear, the main chanting room, to listen to the monks' prayers. After that, we walk around the Vihear and toss the sticky rice on the ground for the spirits who are waiting for their living relatives. After we finish, we go back home.

Pchum Ben is a great time for my family to express the feeling to our ancestors. The festivities begin fourteen days prior to the festival day. Cambodians call these days Dak Ben, offering rice. During these days, my grandparents usually host Dak Ben as often as they can. They take us to visit at least seven temples and give food to ancestors. We believe that food ensures a lot of food for our ancestors. Then, we will have a happy year if our ancestors are happy. Sometimes my family and I go to more than one temple per day. Each day we go farther and farther to temples. Each temple is farther than the previous one. We bring food and fruit to pray for reducing the bad karma of our ancestors. Next, we offer food, fruit, and money to the monks at the Vihear. Then, the monks chant a blessing and shower us with a sprinkle of water. For us, we believe that the blessing and showering will release us and our ancestors from bad luck.

I think this holiday is an amazing traditional holiday in Cambodia. So, I hope this festival will stay forever from one generation to another. I hope that I will celebrate this fascinating holiday again someday.

Days of the Dead
MARILYN MARQUIS

CALIFORNIA HAS A LONG HISTORICAL connection with Mexico. In our early history, California was a Spanish colony. When Mexico gained independence from Spain, California was part of Mexico. California became a territory of the United States in 1848 and soon after became a state, but many counties, cities, and streets still have Spanish names. California also has a very large number of immigrants from Mexico. It is no surprise, then, that some holidays in Mexico are also celebrated here. One of those is The Day of the Dead. Many communities have Day of the Dead celebrations. Even art museums often have special exhibits featuring art and music associated with this holiday.

Halloween has an historical connection with Day of the Dead. Long ago in Europe, the Celtic people believed that on the night before November 1, the souls of all those who died in the previous year gathered to make the passage to the spirit world. That was the beginning of Halloween. The Catholic Church established the holidays of All Saints Day and All Souls Days on November First and Second. These holidays both honor the dead. The Day of the Dead celebration falls on November 1 and 2 and comes from the Catholic Church in Mexico.

Today the Halloween celebration in the United States includes ghosts, ghouls, and goblins, all associated with death. The trick-or-treating traditions probably also have their roots in ancient tradition. In California, we can celebrate both Halloween and the Day of the Dead.

Day of the Dead in Mexico
JUAN VALDEZ

ONE OF THE MOST IMPORTANT holidays in Mexico is the traditional "Day of the Dead". It is celebrated on November First and Second every year. This is a national holiday but the traditions are different in each state. This celebration is important because the families gather together to remember and honor their beloved dead parents and friends. They go to the cemetery and pray for them. They prepare the dead parent's favorite food. They also collect personal items of the person for an altar. When I have the opportunity to join my family for this holiday, I really enjoy being with my relatives and eating the food.

Before the holiday, families plan the ceremony. Members of the family discuss details of the celebration. Each member of the family is responsible for something. For example, somebody brings flowers, another brings drinks, and others bring food. My mother used to cook my grandparents favorite food, like mole, sweet pumpkins, and special bread.

Usually the celebration is held at the cemetery. The families meet there. They clean the gravestones and place some special flowers on them. After that, they gather together and pray for the dead parent's soul. The youngest members of the families usually play and ask a lot of questions about the celebration. Older members talk about the people who died and sometimes sing some favorite songs.

Sometimes the celebration is held at home. People decorate altars with colored paper and flowers. The loved one's picture is placed at the center of the altar, and then some candles are placed in front of the picture. People also place important treasures on the altar. These may include books, musical instruments, and other things the person enjoyed in life. The special food, water, and candies are then placed on the altar. The family usually eats these things after the holiday.

There is a lot of food to eat that day, but this food is just for the spirit of the dead, at least until the end of the celebration. People believe that spirits come to life to eat and drink the food they liked. Families enjoy preparing the favorite meal of their loved ones. The meal always includes bread of the dead, mole, tequila, chicken, rice, and lemonade. At the end of the celebration, families start eating and sharing the food they prepared. Many times they drink the tequila and talk about their ancestors. In addition to the special food, there is special candy made of sugar and chocolate and shaped like little skulls.

Although there are different ways to celebrate this holiday in Mexico, the meaning is the same. Families gather together to remember and honor their loved ones. Families make their best effort to rejoice together with the spirits of their ancestors. All the members of my family know that this is a very special date. My grandparents were very special people in our lives; therefore we celebrate this holiday every year.

Dia de Los Muertos
JOSE TORRES

DIA DE LOS MUERTOS IN Mexico is a very special day. This holiday is celebrated on two days, November First and Second. In this tradition, the spirits come back to our world to visit their families and especially to enjoy traditional food. Our mothers make a beautiful, traditional altar. Then they put a lot of food like tamales, mole, quesadillas, tacos, and enchiladas on the altar. They also include sodas, water, beer, cigarettes, hot chocolate, and anything else the ancestor loved. There is usually a picture of the ancestor as well as flowers, candles, and special candy made of sugar and chocolate in the shape of a skull. People later take the flowers from the altar to the cemetery and they go to church.

After the two days, we can eat all the food and enjoy everything from the altar. I love my culture because it is rich in traditions. I especially love Dia de Los Muertos

CHAPTER SIX
Religious Holidays

Eid
Eid al Fitr in Indonesia
Bathing the Buddha Festival
Trendez, an Armenian Tradition
Festa Junina in Brazil
A Unique Tradition in My Family
Virgin of Guadalupe, Mexico

Religious Holidays

Eid
JAMILA FAROOQI

FOR THE THREE DAYS OF the Eid celebration, all Muslim people have a holiday. It is important to clean the house and buy new clothes for this holiday. Everyone makes cakes and cookies and goes shopping for dried fruit and candies. On the first day of the holiday, all Muslims go to pray, and after prayer, everybody says *Eid mubark* to each other. Women kiss each other and men give big hugs. Some people kiss the children and give them money. All sons and daughters go to visit their parents to pay their respect to their elders. After that, they go to visit their other relatives, sisters, brothers, and friends.

In conclusion, during the Eid celebration, everyone wants to be happy, visit family and friends, drink tea, and eat delicious food: cake, cookies and dry fruit. Everyone is happy in these days, and you find them laughing and enjoying their time. This is a time to forgive and forget.

Eid al Fitr in Indonesia
NOVIEDA TRIKA

I CAME FROM INDONESIA AND MOST of the Indonesian people are Moslem, so Eid al Fitr is the most important religious holiday in our country. This holiday is important for all Indonesian people and influences everyone in the country.

First, a month before Eid al Fitr, Moslems will fast for thirty days. Before fasting, usually Moslems go to the cemetery to visit their ancestors, pay respect, clean up the grave, and put some flowers on the grave. Fasting is a must for the Moslems and begins at daybreak and ends at sunset. People have to control themselves not to eat, drink, get angry, and or do anything inappropriate during this month. The purpose of fasting is to make you a better person.

Second, two weeks before Eid al Fitr, Moslems clean and decorate their houses, neighborhoods, and mosques. They paint their house and make it more beautiful than before. The malls play Islamic music and decorate with green and yellow banners and pictures of *ketupat*. The *ketupat* is a special small woven basket for making rice cakes in Indonesia. All main streets in my city are decorated with colorful banners and twinkle lamps. The office workers also decorate their buildings with banners saying, Happy Eid al Fitr or Celebrate Fasting with the Pure Heart.

It is very crowded everywhere during the weeks before Eid al Fitr because Moslems have to prepare to celebrate the big day. People who go to work usually have their paycheck and holiday bonus earlier than any other month. Then they buy clothes, gifts, and sweets for their children, but they keep them until Eid al Fitr. They also buy cookies, pretzels, and pastry to be served to guests, and sometimes they buy gifts for their business colleagues and friends. The malls are full of people in this season, especially at the gift shops, bakeries, supermarkets, and superstores. Sometimes people will be separated from their family. Often children get separated from their mothers because the mother is so busy with her list.

Next, the last week before the big day, the city becomes more quiet than usual because two-thirds of Moslems will leave for their own hometowns. Because this is an important religious holiday for most Indonesian people, our government makes the whole week a holiday. So the streets are clear, and there is less traffic in the city. People really like this situation because they don't have to rush to go home because there is no traffic. Unfortunately, we still have to be careful of thieves and robberies, especially near the Eid al Fitr.

Finally, the night before Eid al Fitr is the day that the fasting people are waiting for because it is the last day of fasting. After breaking the fast and going to the mosque, usually teenagers and children walk around the neighborhoods. They hit empty plastic bottles together and sing songs about winning the battle against fasting. Main streets are full of Moslems. They are celebrating their victory against the fasting, and sometimes these celebrations cause a traffic jam. Usually these parades start at 8 PM and end at midnight.

On Eid al Fitr, Moslems go to the mosque early in the morning. They wear special clothes to go to the mosque. The women wear a *mukena*. *Mukena* is special praying attire. It is a special white gown from head to foot. The men wear a sarong, a traditional shirt, and *peci* hat. The children also wear new clothes and shoes. After prayers at the mosque, they greet other neighbors quickly and go back home.

There are two days of Eid al Fitr. The first day is for greeting family and asking forgiveness. The first formal greeting starts from their home. Younger people will ask for forgiveness for their bad behavior from their elders. For example, the children will ask forgiveness from their parents. After that, the parents will give their children the gifts that they hid for two weeks. When Moslems visit their older relatives, they get down on their knees and bow to the oldest and ask for forgiveness for what happened in the previous year. Older people usually give money to children when they shake hands. The money ranges between one and ten dollars and depends on the child's age.

The second day they will go on a vacation with their family or visit special places such as the zoo, museum, and playland, beach, or even the mall. If they don't have any place to visit, usually they will wait for friends and colleagues to come to their house.

There are special foods for this holiday. For example, *ketupat* is served with chicken, beef, *chayote* and boiled egg in hot curry. Some people make braised chicken in coconut milk or beef *rendang*, beef cooked in soy sauce. Indonesian vegetables are cooked in coconut curry. For dessert, there is rice, *halwa*, *betawi* or *kolak*, boiled banana, sweet potatoes, and tapioca pearls served in brown sugar syrup and *korma*.

My family is Christian, but when Eid al Fitr comes, my family also cooks and eats *ketupat*. Ketupat is a must for Eid al Fitr and is a tradition in Indonesia. I have many Moslem friends, and when Eid al Fitr comes, I call them and say, *Mohon maaf lahir batin*. It means, "From the bottom of my heart, please forgive all my faults in the previous year." When I go their homes, I also say this to each person in the family. Then we eat delicious foods and desserts. I like this holiday because it is a long holiday, there is no traffic, and I can eat the special foods like *ketupat*.

Bathing the Buddha Festival
KINA CHUNYU

BUDDHISTS AROUND THE WORLD CELEBRATE the birth of Buddha 2,500 years ago with a festival called Bathing the Buddha. The celebration falls on the eighth day of the fourth lunar month. There are Buddhists in many countries, and in each one, the temples celebrate with a Bathing the Buddha Festival. It is a national holiday in Taiwan every year. Every temple will celebrate and provide many special vegetarian dishes for everyone who comes to the ceremony. Bathing the Buddha is one of my favorite holidays.

At the temple, a statue of baby Buddha sits in the center of a bowl on an altar with flowers. The flowers represent the Garden of Lumbini where the Buddha was born. Then monks and nuns recite special prayers, called *sutras*. They then pour fragrant water over the statue to commemorate his birth. They pour water over the Buddha's body, but not on his head. People offer flowers, fruit, candles, and tea to pray for harmony, good health, and world peace. Because the Buddha is the Enlightened One, on the Buddha's birthday there are important things to do. We encourage speaking good words, doing good deeds, and thinking good thoughts. After bathing the Buddha, there are charity events, a food fair, and *dharma* lectures. A *dharma* lecture is a lecture by a Buddhist monk. The monk tells the people how to live a harmonious life and find inner purification.

It is good for parents to bring children to the temple to enjoy the Bathing the Buddha Festival every year.

Trendez, an Armenian Tradition
ARSINEH MANOUKIAN

ONE OF THE ARMENIAN HOLIDAYS is Purification Day. That is called Trendez in Armenian. According to religious custom, this holiday is connected with the idea of coming forward to the Lord with fire forty days after his birth. So the religious name means coming forward to the Lord. The Armenian Church celebrates it on February 14. This is 40 days after January Sixth. The day to celebrate the birth of Jesus is December 25 in most of the western world, but in the Eastern Orthodox church, we celebrate the birth on January Sixth. The main ceremony of Trendez centers around a bonfire, symbolizing the coming of spring. After the ceremonies by the priest in church, people congregate in the church yard and follow the priest to start the big fire. People donate dry grass and tree branches all year and leave it in the church yard. The priest selects two newly married couples to start the fire. The fire must start before the sunset.

We have a lot of traditions for this holiday. For example, if someone starts a new business or someone in the family gets married or has a new child or grandchild, they bring special candy which is made of flour, sugar, butter and many seasonings. When the fire starts, they share and divide the candies among the people. Everyone takes the candies and says thank you and congratulations. People jump on the fire and make a wish. They believe the wish will come true. Many people, who cannot jump on fire, write their wishes on a piece of paper and throw it in the fire. After the fire dies down, people light their candles with that fire. They carry it to their homes and they light a fire with that candle's flame. Sometimes after the church ceremony, families come together in one of their homes and light a fire and eat candies and other food. They are happy because winter is going to go and the warm weather is on the way.

Festa Junina in Brazil
SANDRA KELLING

BRAZILIAN HOLIDAYS ARE FESTIVE AND exciting. One of the more festive holidays is a celebration called Festa Junina, or June Festival. As children, we dressed up like country people, farmers, or hillbillies. We had parties at school and in the town park. We square danced and played games that reminded us of the simpler life that people once had. This holiday is marked by a week-long festival with lots of fun, food, games, dancing, and music. The festival has a history, and it serves to bring people together.

The actual holiday officially happens on June Fifteenth. It is a traditional Catholic celebration in honor of Saint John the Baptist. Festa Junina originated in the hot, dry northern and northeastern states of Pernambuco, Paraiba, Piaui, and Ceara in Brazil. The local people would have a mass and pray to Saint John for rain. Annually, the rainy season begins around June 15, so Festa Junina became a celebration of people's prayers for rain being answered.

To prepare for this week-long event, people get ready all year long. They work on choreography for dances and practice presentations to be given at the festival. Music is selected and practiced for contests. Games are selected, and a master of ceremonies is elected. Small booths and tents are constructed and set up in parks and community centers. Streamers and flags are made to decorate the parks and community centers. Candles and festival lamps are strung together to create a unique and festive atmosphere.

The traditional music of the festival is *forro*, and the traditional dance is called *quadrilha*. *Forro* is very similar to country music found in the United States. *Quadrilha* means square dancing, and it is exactly like the traditional square dancing found in the southern and western United States.

At the festival, people show up dressed like country bumpkins wearing overalls or jeans with suspenders. Everyone wears patches on their clothing. Girls show up with their hair in pigtails, fake freckles on their cheeks, and sometimes a few teeth blackened out. At the costume contest, judges decide who has the most authentic country bumpkin costume.

There is always plenty of food to eat at Festa Junina. You can find *pamonha*, a food somewhat similar to Mexican tamales, and *canjica*, a sweet treat made from hominy. There are also treats like popcorn, cotton candy, peanuts, cakes and fruit punch there.

No festival would be complete without fireworks. Fireworks are shot off during the festival, at various times, but the final show is at the end. It reminds me of the Fourth of July in the United States with a big finale.

One of the games played during the festival is the *correo elegante* or chain of elegance. Someone writes a romantic note, sometimes with funny poetry, and it is passed from person to person like kids passing notes in school. The fun is watching the receiver's response. Sometimes the notes are read from a microphone, and the receiver is given clues to guess who sent the note. This is especially popular with young, single people who need an introduction to someone they want to meet. The biggest show is a bride and groom contest where the judges pick a couple who dress and dance as newlyweds in the most authentic fashion.

Above all of the food and dancing and fun, there is a traditional value to this festival that is easy to miss. To celebrate Festa Junina, people return to the small towns and villages where they were born to meet family and friends. This brings families together, and it is a chance for people to forget their own struggles and problems. For a week, Festa Junina lets us live a fantasy and remember the fun from our childhood.

A Unique Tradition in My Family
RUTH SARMIENTO-ACHULLI

ONE OF THE MOST IMPORTANT unique traditions in my family is Easter because it is a great event for my Catholic family each year. The majority of Catholics in Peru go to church, eat fish, and do not work from Holy Thursday to Easter Sunday. It is considered a very important holiday for Peruvian people because the Catholic religion is the most important religion in Peru.

When I was a child I remembered that I didn't like to celebrate Easter because I couldn't eat until 1 PM on Good Friday. I disliked it very much. My siblings, my cousins and I were bored with that. Every year was the same. We wanted to change it, but we couldn't.

We grew up with one unique Easter tradition in our family. One week before Easter, Palm Sunday, we went to the church. After the mass we bought a palm branch. Then we brought it to the priest for him to bless, and then we took it home. On Holy Thursday, we stayed at home and we watched television programs about the life and death of Christ. We couldn't eat beef, chicken or turkey. We only ate fish. We started to celebrate Easter on Good Friday. We fasted in the morning until 1 PM Then we went to downtown Lima to visit seven churches. We walked all through downtown. We entered each church and we made the sign of the cross. This is a Catholic tradition of using your right hand to touch your forehead, your heart, your left shoulder and then your right shoulder. As you do this you say, "In the name of the Father, the Son and the Holy Spirit, Amen." Then we said a special prayer, The Our Father. At each church, we brought our water for the priest to bless. We kept this holy water in our house all year to bless our home. After visiting the seven churches, we went back home and ate our lunch together. Before eating lunch, we always prayed. It was a special lunch with fish, vegetables, and a lot of food. Later, we rested at home. We watched TV, or we visited our family and relatives.

On Holy Saturday, we didn't do anything special. On Easter Sunday, we went to church to attend mass. Then, we accompanied the procession of the cross in the fourteen stations. After that, my family and I went back home. We ate lunch together. Then, we stayed home. Some of my family rested, and others watched TV. My parents and I visited relatives. After that, we ate a special dinner because it was the last day of Easter. We prayed for our family, relatives, and friends. In these last years, I enjoyed Easter a lot because I was spending more time with my family, relatives, and friends. Also, I felt closer to God. I felt something that I couldn't explain about Easter. It was something wonderful and beautiful. I am very proud of being Catholic.

In conclusion, Easter is a unique tradition and important in my family every year.

Virgin of Guadalupe, Mexico
ANA ALVAREZ

On december 12, people in Mexico honor the Virgin of Guadalupe. This is a religious holiday in a country where most people are Catholic. The celebration begins with a procession from a small parish church to a bigger, main church. People usually walk along the main streets for about four or five miles to get to the big church. An image of the Virgin is always at the front of the procession. People pray, sing happy and religious songs or folkloric songs, and usually there are Indian dances of different tribes. One member of the group has a big drum. That is the only musical instrument. The dances are pretty nice.

After the procession arrives at the main church, people find a place to rest and have something to eat. They spend time with friends and family. Around the church there are many little stores where people can buy food, traditional water, snacks, presents, or religious items. Then all of the people go to church.

A very important part of the celebration is the religious sermon. All the people go into the church to listen to a religious sermon for an hour. The pastor teaches about the Virgin, and then they sing *Happy Birthday* to the Virgin's image at 12 AM, exactly.

When the sermon and singing are over, most people go outside to continue having fun. I really enjoy this celebration. It is a day when people can be with family and friends and at the same time enjoy our religion and our culture. I appreciate the activities we have for the Virgin.

CHAPTER SEVEN
Christmas in Many Lands

Christmas in Bulgaria
Christmas in Burma
Christmas in Colombia
Christmas in El Salvador
When Christmas Begins
Christmas in Nicaragua
My Christmas Memories
Christmas in Ukraine

Christmas in Many Lands

Christmas in Bulgaria
NADEJDA YOSSIFOVA

*I*N THE PAST, WHEN MY father was a child, people strictly followed all of the elements of folk Christmas celebration. One important part of the holiday was the Yule log, called Budnik. It symbolizes the future. The youngest man in the family went into the woods and chose a healthy and fruitful tree. Before cutting it down, he asked for forgiveness. That oak or pear tree was brought home to keep the fire up throughout the night to spread light for the holy mother. According to national beliefs, the Budnik heals and in some regions people used the ashes as a cure or spread them across fields for a good harvest.

The festive Christmas Eve dinner is another exciting part of Christmas in Bulgaria. In the past, a meatless meal was arranged over straw on the floor. This was a reminder of the Nativity of Christ. Today, most Bulgarians sit around the table for a traditional dinner. Every year in my family we used to prepare seven, nine, or twelve dishes. We had stuffed cabbage leaves with rice, bean soup, *oshav*, dried fruits boiled with sugar and spices, ritual bread with a silver coin inside, pastry with pumpkin, boiled wheat, honey, walnuts, and red wine. Everything is symbolic of fertility. Traditionally, Christmas dinner should start early. This will cause the wheat to become ripe earlier. Another tradition says everyone should stay in their seats at the table so the chickens will not leave the nests. The oldest man in the house, my grandfather or father, would ritually break the bread, handing pieces to each family member. The luckiest person got the piece with the coin, signifying success.

The third traditional part in Bulgarian Christmas celebration is the ritual singing of Christmas carols. This usually started at midnight. In the past, the *koledari*, male carol singers, used to go about the houses blessing and singing to the people in the community. They sang for health, happiness, and wealth. People, in turn, gave the *koledari* gifts. They gave small ring-shaped buns, dried fruits, or some money sprinkled with wheat.

These three Bulgarian Christmas traditions reflect the culture of Bulgaria. The holiday and the winter season come together in hopefulness about the future.

Christmas in Burma

YIN YIN SHEIN

PREPARATION BEGINS TWO MONTHS BEFORE Christmas when churches begin practice for the nativity play. In the nativity play, people from the church act the Christmas story with Mary, Joseph, the shepherds, and the three kings. Some churches also collect toys, clothing, food, and different kinds of gifts before Christmas to distribute to the poor. Children also begin preparing before Christmas with wishes for the things they want.

Singing is a very important part of the Christmas season in Burma. Young people practice Christmas songs every Sunday evening before December. It is their favorite time of the year. They start singing carols house to house two weeks before Christmas. All the people welcome the singers at their homes even if they are not Christian. People enjoy listening to the songs and wishing a Christmas wish to each other. The singers enjoy singing the whole night long. It is cool outside but warm in a group of singers.

Some church leaders go to the villages to give a gospel. They conduct games, play the Christmas concert, and give gifts to the villagers. At that time, people are warm with joy and love. Every Christian house in the village or town serves traditional food to the guests. At Christmas, everybody is welcome even without an invitation. People go to their relatives and friends houses and eat all day long. Houses are open for the guests all day, and Christmas music is everywhere.

Christmas in Colombia

MARITZA JOYA

IN SANTA FE DE BOGOTA, the Capital of Colombia, December is the best time to enjoy with family and friends. People celebrate every day and try to stay together on the most important days, Christmas and New Year's.

People start to prepare for the holidays in early December. They feel different from the other months of the year for several reasons. First, something changes in the air. The sky is blue and the light of the sun creates a transparent smooth mist. People breathe the soft cold air that indicates December has arrived with all kinds of feelings: happiness, sadness, life expectancy, memories, and wishes.

Second, working people get an additional payment of around fifteen days of their salary. This is called *prima de navidad*. People are ready to spend it on all the new goods that companies offer at this time of year.

Additionally, the city environment has a big change, too. The employees of the city, businesses, churches, and neighborhoods begin to decorate the streets, the buildings, and the houses with beautiful lights and ornaments related to Christmas. The TV and radio play special music for this time. In conclusion, everything you see, you smell, you touch has the taste of Christmas.

The first celebration is the night of December 7 when outside every house or business people light a candle in the streets to welcome the celebration of the next day, the Immaculate Conception. This is a Catholic holiday which celebrates the purity of Mary, the mother of Jesus. According to the Catholic Church, Mary was born without original sin. This is the sin of Adam and Eve. Catholics go to mass on the feast of the Immaculate Conception and honor the mother of Jesus.

The next important days are December 16 to 24 when people meet in their homes to pray a special novena. A novena is a series of prayers said every day for three or more days. The Christmas novena recalls, through prayer, the journey of Mary and Joseph to Bethlehem before Jesus was born. Together families, friends, and children pray and sing around the nativity scene. The musical instruments for these songs are unique to the season. People use everyday items to make sound, like spoons, *maracas*, metal cans full of grain, and whistles. The hostess offers guests native and traditional snacks. For example, *bunuelos* and *natilla* are the most common. *Bunuelos* are little dark yellow fried balls made with flour dough mixed with cheese. *Natilla* is a dessert made with milk, corn flour, brown sugar, and cinnamon. People also prepare a soft liquor drink called *sabajon*. It is made with condensed milk, cream, and *Aguardiente*, native liquor. According to custom, each day is celebrated in a different house. Recently the malls or clubhouses in big buildings are inviting people in their neighborhoods to celebrate these days.

The most important family day is December 24 when families meet to celebrate the birth of Jesus. Most people celebrate Christmas at their parents' or grandparents' houses. Children are the most important people in this celebration. Everything is to enjoy with them. Families arrive at the parents' house between 7 and 10 PM. They bring their gifts and put them around the Christmas tree. Sometimes, before midnight, people spend time talking, lighting fireworks, dancing, and eating small snacks. At 11:30 the whole family gathers around the nativity scene to pray and sing for the last day of the novena. The prayers must finish before 11:50 when the family sings until twelve o'clock. Then they start to hug each other and say happy

Christmas. It is wonderful. Sometimes emotional tears slide down the faces of the old people in the family, but it is time to smile and feel happiness. Everyone sits around the Christmas tree. Finally the time to share our gifts has arrived. One or two of the children are selected to read the labels of the gifts and hand out gifts. The faces show the expectations and happiness at each gift. Children are especially joyful when the sender of the gift is Baby Jesus. Children sometimes send letters to Baby Jesus asking for a special toy. When they receive the gift from Baby Jesus, children and their parents feel a special excitement.

After the gifts are given and received, dinner is served. The most common dish in Bogota is *ajiaco*. This is a delicious potato and chicken soup. People also enjoy *tamales*, chicken, or pork inside seasoned corn dough and wrapped with fresh green leaves. Sometimes people dance until 4 or 5 AM. The next day, people meet again to have dinner and enjoy Christmas day. Also, they usually go to mass in the morning.

The last celebration of December comes a week later. December 31 is the meeting of the old year and new year. This celebration is less formal than December 24, Christmas Eve. People share this holiday with friends, too. The oldest daughter in the family usually invites everyone to her house for the celebration. Nicely dressed guests start to arrive after 10 PM. The dinner table is already decorated with wine glasses, champagne bottles, plates with twelve grapes on each one, and some snacks. Sometimes people dance while waiting for 11:55, when everyone starts the countdown to midnight. At that moment of finishing the old year and welcoming the new year, people hug and kiss, wishing best wishes to one another for the new year. Then someone makes a toast, and everyone eats the twelve grapes for good luck. Outside on the streets, people are lighting fireworks. The sound is tremendous, and the sky looks bright with the multiple colors and shapes of the fireworks.

The New Year's celebration closes the most important month of the year and closes all the chapters in the life of the old year. It is time for optimism to begin the New Year with all new chapters in the book of our life.

Christmas in El Salvador
DEYSI M MARTINEZ

PREPARATION FOR CHRISTMAS BEGINS IN early December. People decorate their homes on the inside as well as the outside with wreaths, lights, and deer. People put a pine tree in the corner of the living room or in front of a window.

Christmas has two traditions in El Salvador. The first is the children's story of Santa Claus. On December 24, Santa Claus comes in all the houses at midnight. He brings presents to the good children, especially the good children who have good behavior with their parents, family, and friends. The other is the birthday of Jesus. In El Salvador, at exactly midnight someone puts the baby Jesus under the Christmas tree.

The excitement begins on December Twenty-fourth. In the morning on Christmas Eve, I get up early to wrap the presents for family and friends. In the afternoon, I help my mother with the last preparations for a special, delicious dinner of turkey, chicken, fried rice, vegetable salad, fruit salad, dessert, and a special drink like punch. In the evening, family and friends arrive. The celebration begins with snacks like cookies, tortillas with cheese, and different drinks. Everyone enjoys talking with each other before eating the big dinner. Before dessert is served, all the adults leave the table and put the presents under the Christmas tree. Then the adults call the children and ask the children if they want to see Santa Claus. All the children hope to see Santa. When they do not see Santa, the children feel a little disappointed. When they see the presents, however, they forget those feelings quickly.

When everyone finishes opening their presents, we go back to the table for a special dessert. After dessert, the children play with their new toys, and the adults sit in the living room for a long time. We enjoy talking and drinking together until very late. Christmas Eve is my favorite holiday because I like to spend time with family and friends.

When Christmas Begins
MARTHA ORTIZ

WHEN DECEMBER BEGINS AND CHRISTMAS is right around the corner, we begin to decorate the walls, windows, and the front door with colorful lights and little ornaments. We put a big wreath on our front door. Inside my house, we put a natural pine tree and decorate it with lights, colorful ornaments, and a big star on the top. Our Christmas tree always goes in front of our window, so other people can see it as they walk by our house. Christmas for my family and me has two different meanings. The first meaning is the religious one. Christmas is said to be the day when Jesus was born and we celebrate his birth. The second meaning of Christmas is the story of Santa Claus. Santa Claus is a fat jolly man who gives presents to the good boys and girls. The bad boys and girls get sacks of coal. This story is told to our little children so that they will behave the whole year. Otherwise, they would receive a sack of coal for Christmas instead of toys.

Christmas evening is spent receiving guests at our house. Each guest brings a dish of food, for example, tamales, *posole*, or *ponche*. all of which are authentic Mexican food. When everyone has arrived, we all sit around the table to have dinner. Before we eat, we must say a prayer for the birth of Jesus. When we all finish eating, we begin to dance. Some begin to drink tequila, while others prefer to start a conversation. The children play. Then they are sent to bed so that Santa Claus can stop by and leave them their toys. The children open their toys early the next morning, and begin to play with them.

Christmas in Nicaragua
JENNIFER SUMMERS

THE UNIQUE CHRISTMAS CELEBRATION IN Managua, Nicaragua, has some interesting differences from the ways of celebrating in the United States. Christmas is a time of happiness and rejoicing with families and neighbors in a large celebration on December 24 with fireworks, new clothes, and special food.

On the twenty-fourth of December, people in Nicaragua light fireworks every six hours from 6 AM to midnight, a total of four times in the day. People in the neighborhood enjoy seeing and hearing the fireworks. People of all ages and genders can light the fireworks. Unfortunately, it is also dangerous and many young people and adults are killed or injured during the holidays.

For Christmas, people do not wear cultural costumes, but it is a tradition for most people to buy new clothes, new shoes, and even to get a haircut to look nice.

A few hours before dinner, people decorate the table with candles, cakes, and fruits. The special Christmas dish is called *pollo relleno*. This is chicken stuffed with vegetables, potatoes, raisins, celery, carrots, and many other ingredients. We also add rice on the side with a piece of white bread. This dish is eaten only on Christmas and the New Year.

After dinner, people relax and dance in the house, waiting for the clock to strike 12 AM. The children are impatient to open the presents that baby Jesus brought for them. At midnight, everyone wishes each other Merry Christmas and gives each other a hug and a kiss. Then we sing Christmas songs and light fireworks for about an hour. I will never forget that time of happiness.

My Christmas Memories
MARILYN MARQUIS

SOME OF MY FONDEST MEMORIES of childhood are of Christmas. Our family traditions included a blend of my mother's Italian family and American traditions. In the United States, most families combine national and religious traditions from their ancestors with typical American traditions. My family is Roman Catholic. My mother's parents were from Italy and my father's mother's family was from Ireland. His father's family came to the United States in early 1700 from England, so they are very American.

We began our preparations with the advent season four weeks before Christmas, so the excitement built slowly. We decorated our house, both inside and out. My father made a wooden Santa on his sleigh with a reindeer. He and my older brother painted Santa in a bright red suit with a long white beard. Every year they climbed up on the roof to place the Santa, sleigh, and reindeer in a prominent position. Then they put colorful lights along the roof and in some plants outside the house. Many families in our neighborhood also placed colorful decorations on their roofs and in the plants, so our street looked beautiful for several weeks every December.

My mother made decorations for inside the house. She made a cookie jar one year by using a clear glass bowl. She decorated a plastic ball to look like Santa and used it as a lid. It had a happy face, a long white beard, and a red Santa hat. This cookie jar was filled with my favorite cookies. They were delicious little pecan cookie balls covered with powdered sugar. They looked very tempting in the cookie jar, and I was often caught with my hand in the jar or with powdered sugar on my hands and mouth. These are still my favorite cookies and I look forward to Christmas every year when I make them myself.

Our Christmas tree was usually the last one in the neighborhood to have decorations. When we were very young, Santa decorated the tree after we were asleep. Later our family decorated the tree together on Christmas Eve. My father began the event by testing the string of lights first and then carefully placing them on the tree. After that, we opened the boxes of beautifully crafted glass ornaments. My mother taught us to hang the ornaments with great care because they broke easily. They seemed very valuable to us because they were old and not replaceable. The value came from seeing them on the tree year after year and learning to appreciate their importance in our family tradition. Of course, every year we broke one or two and felt sad at the sound of a crushed glass ball or bell.

Once the ornaments were on the tree to my mother's satisfaction, she carefully hung tinsel. Tinsel is no longer a popular decoration on Christmas trees, but all through my childhood the silver strands of aluminum foil hung in singular elegance on every branch of the tree. The silver reflected the colors of the lights and looked beautiful.

Our tree was usually up long after the other families took down their Christmas decorations. We always kept all of the decorations until January Sixth. My mother called this Little Christmas. In Italian tradition, Bufana brings a small gift to the children. This symbolized the gifts of the three wise men, the three kings, to baby Jesus. In some cultures January 6 is celebrated as Twelfth Night, and in others, it is called Three Kings' Day. For our family, it was the day to take down the Christmas decorations because the holiday season was over.

Christmas cards are another lovely tradition. They help us to keep in touch with family and friends and to extend good wishes for a happy holiday season. In my family my father always addressed the cards. He had beautiful handwriting. I have fond memories of sitting beside him as he addressed the envelopes and signed the cards. He took great pride in making each name look elegant. His father before him did the same. My father also had the honor of opening every card. After the mail arrived, my mother placed the important mail in a small tray. Christmas cards were very important mail. My father opened each one and then we placed the cards in the living room and dining room as decorations to add to the festive holiday mood.

Christmas Eve was the most exciting day of the year. After dinner we all sat in the living room to receive our gifts. We each gave gifts to everyone in the family and placed them under the tree. Our family lived in California, but most of our relatives lived in Chicago, Illinois. They mailed presents to us to open on Christmas Eve. The sight of the decorated tree with piles of wrapped gifts excited the imagination of us all.

My father picked up each wrapped package and read the tag aloud: "To Greg. From Uncle Eddie and Aunt Lori." "To Pam. From Poppy." We sat in silent anticipation as each one opened the gift. Then we looked politely as we waited to hear our own name to receive a gift. When the gifts were all opened, we cleared away the piles of colorful paper and ribbon and we each made a small pile of Christmas treasures under the tree. After we hung our stockings, we put on our new pajamas. We always received new pajamas from our parents. Then we went to bed with hope for a very special gift from Santa.

On Christmas morning my brothers, sister, and I awoke early. We waited until we were all awake, and then we made enough noise to wake our parents. Finally, we all went to the living room to see what Santa left for us. Later we put on our new clothes and went to church. The choir sang beautiful carols, and the church was decorated with large baskets of flowers. We always felt excited about seeing the nativity scene on Christmas morning because the baby Jesus was in his straw bed. After mass we went home to play with our new toys. Mom made dinner early on Christmas. She also set the table with a special tablecloth and napkins and her most beautiful dishes and glasses. The table looked beautiful. We often had turkey with mashed potatoes and gravy, sweet potatoes, vegetables, and cranberry sauce. This meal was very similar to Thanksgiving dinner.

We lived in southern California where a typical Christmas day was sunny with blue sky and warm air. We rode our new bicycles, roller skates, or scooters, or played ball with the other neighborhood children. As evening came, we went inside to play games or change the clothes on our new dolls.

These are lovely memories of Christmases past. My own children will have a different story to tell. I hope theirs will hold as much pleasure as mine.

Christmas in Ukraine

YANA LAUER

ONE OF THE MOST INTERESTING parties in Ukraine is the Christmas celebration on January Sixth and Seventh. People look forward to celebrating this holiday all year. They prepare their houses and a Christmas tree and cook traditional dishes. I liked the celebration very much and celebrated every year when I lived in Ukraine. We had dinner with family and friends.

We have some unique traditions in Ukraine. Dinner on January 6 begins with the first star in the sky. The first dish had to be *kutja*, made of wheat, poppy seeds, and honey. Traditionally, there should be twelve lean dishes on the table, but not every family honors this tradition. Now people usually make their favorite dishes. For example, I usually cook a variety of salads, potatoes and meat or fish.

Later that evening, children in the neighborhood visit every house. They knock on the door and say, "Can we come in?" and each family invites them in. The children tell stories, recite poems, or sing a Christmas song. When they finish, the children receive candy or money. During the evening many children and some adults stroll through the neighborhood to visit each house. The adults often prefer alcohol for their songs or poetry.

After midnight, some people like to tell fortunes. Sometimes my friends and I would try to see our fortunes. It was quite interesting. Each one took some paper, crumpled it up, and put it on a plate. Then we turned off all the lights and set the paper on fire. After the paper burned, each one held the plate and turned around near a wall so we could see some shadows on the wall. The figures that we saw would tell our future. For example, one year my friend saw the shadow of a woman in a long dress with a long veil. That year she got married.

In the afternoon on the next day, people walk along the main street. Even though the temperature is often 5 degrees below zero, people are out for the activities. There is always a big Christmas tree in the middle of the town square. There are also merry-go-rounds for the children to play on. Vendors sell candy and cotton candy on the street. Usually there is a horse and buggy so people can take a short ride along the street. Groups of singers fill the air with songs about Christmas, and musicians play traditional instruments, like *bandura*, *balalaika*, *bayan*, and little bells. Many people wear traditional clothes, wide red pants, warm sheepskin coats, and sheepskin hats. This is always a very festive occasion.

Everyone likes Christmas. In Ukraine, people enjoy being with their families and friends, going door to door to recite poems and sing songs, and the festive activities. Christmas brings warmth to our hearts and hope for the coming year.

CHAPTER EIGHT
Independence Day

July 4th Memories
Independence Day in Mexico
A Parade and Fireworks
Celebrate with Feelings
Banda Bou Day in Curacao
Mali Independence
Independence Day in Indonesia?

Independence Day

July 4th Memories
SARAH NIELSEN

As a child, I used to love celebrating Fourth of July, the Independence Day of the United States. The week before Fourth of July celebrations, my cousins and I decorated our bicycles. With great care, we threaded red, white, and blue crepe paper through the spokes of our tires. With our clumsy kid hands, we cut red, white, and blue construction paper into thin strips to make streamers to attach to our handle bars. With thick, heavy pencils, we drew the stars and stripes of the United States flag on white paper. After that, we colored our flags in with red, white, and blue crayons and attached those flags to the back of our seats.

While my cousins and I were busy decorating our bicycles, our mothers were busy sewing festive red, white, and blue dresses for us. "Stand up straight! Stand still!" our mothers told us, as they checked the length of our dresses, and pinned up the hems to sew by hand later. It was hard to stand still during those fittings for our Fourth of July clothes. We were excited and restless. We were impatient to ride our bikes and wear our special clothes in the big Fourth of July parade.

When the Fourth of July finally arrived, my cousins and I rode our decorated bicycles with other young children in the parade in our town. We pedaled hard to keep up with the marching bands, baton twirlers, and patriotic floats. We felt special, like movie stars, as we waved and smiled at the spectators watching the parade.

After the parade, hot and tired, we went home to swim in the cool waters of the creek behind our house. Later in the day, we had a Fourth of July barbecue with hamburgers, hot dogs, potato salad, and watermelon. Near dusk, all the kids and adults piled into cars to drive to the big public park in town to watch the firework display. We found the perfect spot in the park to spread out blankets, stretch out on our backs, and wait for the fireworks to begin. Before long, music started to play on scratchy speakers, and the sky lit up with red, white, and blue bursts. The fireworks came loud and fast as my cousins and I said, "Ooh! Aah! Did you see that one? Wow!"

When the fireworks were done, our family piled back into our cars. There was a giant traffic jam leaving the park. For my parents, aunts and uncles, this must have been very frustrating. For my cousins and me, the traffic jam meant drifting to sleep in the car, dreaming of riding our bicycles in the parade under the bright lights of the fireworks. When we arrived home, my dad and uncles carried each sleepy kid into the house, gently putting us into bed where more Fourth of July dreams waited.

Now as an adult, I know more about the history of the Fourth of July. I know more about the ways the United States does not live up to the ideals our founding fathers expressed when they declared our independence from England. Sometimes, I miss my innocence and those carefree Fourth of July days of my childhood.

Independence Day in Mexico

MARIA ELENA BELTRAR

TODAY MEXICAN INDEPENDENCE DAY IS a major celebration in Mexico. It is bigger than Cinco de Mayo. The people of Mexico celebrate with a fiesta. Fiestas can be simple or elaborate, and it can last from one day up to a week or more. The fiestas include listening to music, dancing, eating spicy food, drinking strong drinks, as well as watching bullfights, rodeos, and fireworks.

The celebrating begins on September 15, the eve of Independence Day. People in cities, towns, and villages gather together on this day. In Mexico City, they decorate the city with flags, flowers, and lights of red, white, and green. Red, white, and green are the national colors of Mexico. The people also eat lots of food. The people watch the time, and when the clock strikes eleven o'clock, the crowds grow silent.

On the last strike of eleven o'clock on September 15, the president of Mexico steps out onto the balcony, and rings the historic liberty bell that Father Hidalgo rang to call the people. The president shouts "Viva Mexico" (long live Mexico) and "Viva la Independencia" (long live independence), and the crowds echo back with their own patriotic cries. While the crowds shout, the air fills with confetti, streamers, and noise. The day of September 16 is similar to July 4 in the United States. There are statues in memory of Father Hidalgo, and people decorate the statues with red, white, and green flowers.

This is the way we celebrate our Independence Day in Mexico. As a Mexican, I'm proud of our national tradition. Family and friends get together on September 16. We make a lot of food and play a lot of games for all of us to enjoy. There's a special dance I enjoy with my family and friends. The dance is called dances-with-swords. This dance delights both children and adults.

A Parade and Fireworks
JAVIER ESPARZA

I USED TO CELEBRATE INDEPENDENCE DAY with my friends. In my city, we have a huge parade. We also have a special tradition to get together in the city at night to listen to mariachi music. Fireworks are also traditional on this day.

The parade begins on the north side of the city, and it continues for two miles through the city. Some people wear costumes and follow the parade all the way to the end. Other people just like to watch the parade pass by because sometimes it is difficult to walk among all the people following the parade.

Mariachi music is a very important part of Independence Day. During the night, many people get together in the city to celebrate and dance to mariachi music. It is legal to have a drink during this holiday because I believe that the police officers are celebrating as well.

Fireworks are always wonderful, but on September 15 in my city, they are super great. In fact, people from Japan and other countries come to celebrate the day with their fireworks. It is amazing because sometimes firework displays will last two hours straight without stopping.

I like to celebrate Independence Day in my city because I get together with my best friends and have fun. But the most important reason I like this holiday is because I love my country. I like the history behind it, and independence is part of it.

Celebrate with Feelings
NARDA DIAZ PONCE DE LEON

THE MOST IMPORTANT HOLIDAY IN my country, Peru, is Independence Day, held on July Twenty-eighth. Our independence from Spain was declared on July 26, 1824, by the liberator Jose de San Martin. On Independence Day, people have two days off. It is a national celebration throughout Peru.

Usually on this holiday, every worker receives double the regular salary for July. Some companies will pay their workers even more money. The people are happy to celebrate this holiday.

On July 27, the president first gives a speech in Congress to the nation. Most of the time, he gives good news to the nation. The next part of the celebration is a parade of civil and military delegations such as the air force, army, navy, and schools. Public delegations and the civilian population also participate in the parade. The firefighters are always at the tail end of the parade procession. In Lima, the capital of Peru, the parade lasts three or four days, and almost all Peruvian states have a parade for at least two days. Often the celebration is longer, beginning on July 27 and continuing through July 31, the last day of the month.

Besides the presidential speech and the parades throughout the country, families enjoy the holiday and have fun together. Some of them travel to the interior of the country. It was the most important and longest holiday for me, and I think that is true for almost all people in Peru. I looked forward to Independence Day every year. I used to travel to the interior and visit new cities in my country. In fact, I have been to 22 of the 24 Peruvian states.

Peruvians celebrate the anniversary of independence from Spain with great patriotic feelings throughout the country. Flags fly high and the fun starts the night before the official ceremonies with dancing and folk music filling all the city's parks and plazas. There are also bullfights, fireworks, exhibitions and fairs. At the fairs, there are national products and indigenous food and crafts. The best thing I remember is all the music in the plazas and public parks. Many famous national and international singers perform there.

Finally, I can tell you about the next morning. At dawn on July 28, there is a twenty-one cannon salute to herald the ceremony of raising the Peruvian flag. After dancing, drinking, and generally enjoying themselves all night on July 27, many people miss the patriotic celebration on July 28 because they are sleeping!

Banda Bou Day in Curaçao

NURU MITCHUM

THE ISLAND OF CURAÇAO HAS a rich mixture of races and cultures from Dutch, Portuguese, Spanish, African, Jewish and Asian people. Because Curaçao has such a rich cultural diversity, the country also has a full calendar of holidays and festivals including Carnival, Curaçao Day, Rosh Hashanah, Antillean Day, and Saint Nicolas Day, just to name a few. Out of these holidays, I have a favorite holiday that shows the history and culture of our island.

My favorite holiday is called Banda Bou Day, and it occurs on October 1. Banda Bou is the first liberated slave settlements of the Caribbean islands. On Banda Bou Day, inhabitants of Curaçao Island's western region of Banda Bou join other ethnicities to celebrate their history.

Preparations for the Banda Bou Day happen all year long. A committee forms and elects a chairperson to lead the preparations. Local residents and business owners contribute all year long to the event. Farmers, growers, and butchers contribute food to the festival. Regional schools and local community groups prepare dance performances for the holiday. Banners and decorations show historical images of slavery. An older community member is chosen to tell the stories of the local history. This telling of the local history marks the beginning of the festival.

At the festival, there is authentic local food found only on Banda Bou Day. These foods include *erwen*, a thick pea soup made with ham and pork sausage, and *nasi goring*, bean sprouts sautéed with chunks of meat and chicken. There is also *bami*, a long noodle with vegetables and meat, *sate*, skewered meat with peanut sauce, and *rijsttafel*, rice served with up to twenty-five side dishes. We also like to have vegetables like cucumbers combined with green papaya, or cabbage stewed with pickled onions. Of course, there are sweets, such as *sunchi-meringue*, or what we call kisses made of sugar, egg whites, and food coloring, and *panseikeu*, a kind of praline made from toasted peanuts and almond essence, cooked in a brittle glaze of dark brown sugar. There is also *kokada*, freshly grated coconut patties, held together in sugar syrup and tinted with food coloring.

The festival's music is very captivating. The most influential Banda Bou Day music and dance descends from Africa. My favorite music is called Tumba. It is one of the most important forms of local Curaçao music and shows the African influence. We dance in a big group to this fast drum music. Other music is played that includes foreign traditional music such as Merengue, Calypso, Salsa, and Cha Cha. At this celebration, I used to eat and dance all day.

Banda Bou Day is rich in culture and history. The festival activities are very organized and make the holiday very special. The day is marked by good food, great music, and enjoyable dancing. This is the only holiday I participate in often, and I plan on taking future vacations to Curaçao to attend every year that I can.

Mali Independence
MOULAYE C. KEITA

NATIONAL INDEPENDENCE IS AN IMPORTANT step for a group of people living under the authority of another country. For different reasons, powerful countries of the world invade less powerful countries and gain control of the government. The day those less powerful countries get their freedom is generally saved as a very important holiday. Mali, the largest country in West Africa, gained independence from France on September 22, 1960, after many years of occupation and struggle.

The Malian people have a unique way of celebrating their independence. Festivities start at least a week before the big day. Everyone is very excited, and everywhere people are talking about Independence Day. People talk about what they did last year and what they plan to do this year.

People also use this time to review the political changes over the last year. Students learn about the history of Mali independence. Parents teach their children about the Malian struggle for freedom. Students also learn the meaning of our national anthem. Our anthem was composed by an important politician and novelist, Seydou Badian Kouyet. Our first president, Modibo Keita, requested this.

Excitement grows and the day approaches. Soldiers get ready for the parade and most young people get ready for parties. This is a useful time as well as a fun time. It is when we have new hairstyles and new clothes. It is a time of innovation.

Independence Day in Indonesia

EDWARD FRANSINDANI

ALL COUNTRIES IN THE WORLD have many different holidays. My country, Indonesia, has many religious holidays from Moslem, Christian, Hindu, and Buddhist traditions. But, the most important holiday in my country is Independence Day. We celebrate on August 17 every year. This is a formal and historic holiday because we celebrate the memory of the hard work of previous leaders. They worked hard to gain independence for our government. It was not easy to gain independence from the Netherlands and Japan. We had to fight wars and struggle for a long time. The war was not over until the end of World War II.

Now every year on August 17, we celebrate our freedom. A week before the celebration, many people display the national flag in their homes. The celebration begins with a funeral to honor the dead. Ceremonies are at the President's palace, at schools and at offices. After the funeral, there are many competitions for young people. These include towing rope, climbing oily pinang trees, sack racing, and even eating competitions. People enjoy watching these events.

For this holiday we do not have special food, clothing, or decorations. We do not give or receive gifts. We celebrate those who died for our country and enjoy our freedom.

CHAPTER NINE
Unique Holidays

Pongal Festival
Saint Andrew's Day Eve in Poland
Pancake Week in Russia
Chung Yang Festival
Valentine's Day in China
Hanami
Adult Pledge Ceremony
Coming of Age Day
A Family Tradition

Unique Holidays

Pongal Festival
KALYANI SRINIVASAN

THE PONGAL FESTIVAL IS A traditional and cultural holiday in my country, India. In fact, it is a three-day national holiday. Because India is a developing country, most people live in small villages and make their living by farming. In other words, agriculture is an important way of life. In some ways, the Pongal Festival is similar to the USA's Thanksgiving. People who live in a town give thanks to the farmers and agriculture. The farmers themselves thank the sun, which helps them grow the crops in their fields. We believe the sun is God because it helps the farmers a lot.

The Pongal Festival is celebrated on January 14, 15, and 16 every year. Before January, farmers harvest their rice plants and have new rice at home. One month before the Pongal Festival, we start to clean and decorate our house. We decorate the house with mango leaves, and we make dots with sandalwood powder and *kumkum*, a red colored powder, for the house doors. We also decorate with pictures of God. We make drawings with rice flour for the front of the house and for the stove.

On the first day of the festival, we cook in the open air. All the family members are in the open air together, and we make sweet rice and salt and pepper rice. To make the rice, we put rice and water in a large open pot. As the rice cooks, the bubbling water will come out of the open pot. At that time, just for fun, we can shout two or three times, "PONGAL! PONGAL!" After that, we pray to the sun, and we eat together.

The second day of the Pongal Festival is for all the cows and bulls. These animals also help us earn our living, so it is important to give our thanks to them. First thing in the morning, we clean and decorate their pens. After that, we give them a shower and put makeup on them. We also paint their horns and put flower necklaces around their necks. Finally, we put dots made of sandalwood powder on their faces and tails. At noon, we cook sweet rice and feed it to them. In the evening, ranchers take their cows and bulls to a big, open field to eat grass.

The third day of the Pongal Festival is for friends and relatives to see each other and socialize. During the first two days of the festival, we have many activities. On the third day, we can relax a little. Sometimes distant relatives and friends will come to our house, or we go to their houses to talk or watch movies. The Pongal Festival is very important for us.

Saint Andrew's Day Eve in Poland

ALINA DITTMANN

As winter approaches, the days get shorter, and the nights get longer and colder. In Central Europe, people look for entertainment to make the long dark evenings brighter and warmer. In Poland, at the end of November young men and women prepare for this special holiday. On November 29, we celebrate Saint Andrew's Day. This holiday is not unique to Poland. People in Sweden, Russia, and Greece also celebrate this holiday. It is always the sign that Advent is coming soon. The first Sunday of Advent begins the time of spiritual reflection and prayers before Christmas.

The name of the event comes from Saint Andrew, the patron saint of Sweden, Russia, and Greece. He was one of the Apostles and was crucified on November 30, in the year 70. But the celebration is not about him now. In modern times, the celebration brings young women and men together. It also includes some pre-Christian traditions. For example, the Slavic influence includes dancing and fortune-telling. Some special rituals give people some ideas about their future in the coming year.

The main ritual of the fortune-telling and divination of the future is pouring wax through a big old key into cold water and interpreting the shadow of the wax shape on a wall. One other future prediction is called a shoegame. This game is played by unmarried women who take their left shoe off. Each young woman places her shoe in a line. As each shoe is added, the line of shoes gets closer to the main door of the house. The shoe that crosses the threshold of the door has special meaning. That shoe shows who will get married first in the new year.

Most of the games and fortune-telling are about relationships, marriage, and love. For example, in one game, a walnut shell with a burning candle in a bowl of water can predict lasting love. The bowl of water has one walnut shell with a burning candle. A young woman then sets her walnut shell with a burning candle into a bowl of water. She thinks of her boyfriend as she places the nutshell. If her nutshell reaches the other nutshell, her love will never die. If they float away from each other, the relationship will not last.

In another game, the cupgame, four cups each have something hidden underneath. A wedding ring is under one cup. A coin is under another. A leaf is under the third cup. The fourth cup has nothing. Each of these items has a special meaning. The wedding ring means marriage. The coin means material wealth. The leaf means love will appear. The empty cup means the next year will not bring changes. Each person chooses a cup to tell her future.

These games come from a long history of late fall with very long evenings and nothing special to do. Villagers gathered together to tell stories and arrange marriages. They distract people from the cold November wind. Today Saint Andrew Evening has dancing, eating, and flirting. It also brings the hope of new romance to warm the long, cold, lonely winter months.

Pancake Week in Russia
VIKTORIYA SMIRNOVA

THERE ARE OVER TWO HUNDRED countries in the world. All of them are different and have their own history and traditions. Mostly all of them take care of their customs and celebrations which came from ancient ages. Russia is one of them. It is a country with an old culture which is passed down from older generations to younger ones. These cultural traditions came from different kinds of people and different historical times. Eventually, they were accepted and combined together. Even though the country changed a lot, Russian people try to keep their traditions and historical customs. One of these which we continue to celebrate with pleasure is pancake week.

Pancake week is an old Russian holiday which is over a thousand years old. The whole week is assigned to that celebration. It is an old Slavonic, heathen holiday to say goodbye to the winter, and was celebrated on the vernal equinox — March Twenty-first. The Orthodox Church retained this spring holiday in order to not reject the Russian tradition. However, they moved the time of the holiday so it did not conflict with Lent.

Pancake week is a mischievous and merry farewell to winter and greeting to spring which brings the waking up of nature and sunny warmth. Since the beginning of time people connect spring to the beginning of new life. In ancient times, they honored the sun for giving life and strength to everything living. A long time ago, to honor the sun, people cooked pancakes and believed that the round pancakes, which looked like the sun, gave them warmth and power. Merriment and people's parties continued through pancake week. People indulged in different kinds of fun:

tobogganing, preposterous shows of buffoonery, driving horse-drawn sleds, carnivals, fistfights, and noisy excursions into the city or village. Usually on Wednesday, families visited their maternal mother-in-law, and she treated them to pancakes. Pancakes are baked differently, thin or thick, served with honey, jam, sour cream, meat, or caviar.

The last day of pancake week is pardon day. On this day, a straw man, as a symbol of winter, is burned. Winter disappears like the straw man. Everyone asks for forgiveness from each other. They hope to be free of sins. When people ask for forgiveness, we reply, "God absolves."

Keeping and sharing ancient traditions can be useful and enjoyable for the modern people. Russians enjoy sharing this one.

Chung Yang Festival
YU JIE LIU

CHUNG YANG FESTIVAL IS ALSO known as Double Nine Festival in China. According to Chinese astronomy, the number nine is associated with Yang, the sun. Yang is important in Chinese culture. Therefore, on the ninth day of the ninth month on the Chinese lunar calendar, Chinese people have the Chung Yang Festival. Chung means double in Chinese. This is a traditional holiday in China.

This holiday, like many Chinese holidays, reveals the Chinese concept of family. On this day people think of and miss the family members who passed away, but this is different from Qing Ming, the day we honor ancestors. For Chung Yang, people usually set up a table full of food for praying to the ancestors in the morning at home. The other activities are outdoor fun.

Chung Yang Festival is also a fun holiday because people do many interesting things that day. For example, people like to go hiking. My family's tradition was to go hiking at midnight for about an hour and a half in the hills near our house. Even though it was midnight, there were many people also hiking at that time. It was quite a lively time. Roadside stores were open along the path. After our hike, my family had a late-night dinner. We always ate *dim sum*. The children of the family have great fun because no one asks them to go to sleep.

During the day, many people also like to fly kites. That is one of my favorite activities of Chung Yang Festival. The children not only fly kites, but they also use the kites to battle other kites. It works like this: We fly the kites near other kids with their kites. Then we attempt to cut between the others' string connected to kites by using the string of our kites. When we are successful, the other kites go down. At the end of the day, we will see whose kites can last the longest time in the sky. That person is the king of kites for the day.

Another activity of the festival is viewing chrysanthemums. We enjoy the blooming of chrysanthemums in the parks. On September the ninth the flower reaches the full bloom of the season. The chrysanthemum is a famous flower. Many Chinese love it because it represents heroic gentlemen. In the movie, *The Course of the Golden Flower*, that golden flower is a chrysanthemum and the golden flower festival in the movie is Chung Yang Festival.

Chung Yang Festival is a fascinating holiday. People have lots of fun hiking, flying kites, and enjoying flower viewing. Yet it is also a profound holiday remembering the family members who are no longer with us.

Valentine's Day in Japan
YUKIKO EGAWA

UNLIKE IN THE USA, ONLY women give their sweethearts chocolate on Valentine's Day in Japan. Traditionally, Japanese women are quiet and do not express their feeling to men directly. On Valentine's Day, however, they can show their feelings openly to men. This is a modern tradition in Japan. In the 1960's, some very clever marketing staff in a Japanese chocolate company made a catchy commercial. It targeted young women. It said, "Give a box of chocolates to your special person, and express your passion on February 14, Valentine's Day, ." It caught many young women's hearts, and it became an annual tradition. Modern Japanese women are not always passive and do not follow the men's shadow like the ladies a hundred years ago in Japan, but Valentine's Day has romantic meaning among young women.

When I was a middle school student, Valentine's Day was a very special day for us. Many girls carefully selected gift chocolate and wrote love letters to their crushes. We made strategies about how to give presents to them. Some of them gave chocolate openly in front of the other classmates, but most of us were more careful not to embarrass their sweethearts. Usually, soccer or baseball players were popular among girls, so they received a lot of chocolate. At that time, giving and receiving Valentine's chocolate was a serious event, so both boys and girls were a little nervous on that day. I'm sure that most Japanese people have some kind of heartwarming memory on Valentine's Day.

The chocolate for a real love is *honmei-choco*. Is it for just one special person. However, nowadays women buy a lot of chocolate for Valentine's Day and give some *giri-choco*, obligation chocolate, to their male bosses, colleagues and classmates.

For marketing purposes, another Japanese chocolate company introduced a unique custom. Japan has a group culture, and harmony is more important than individual will. Breaking harmony is the last thing to expect in Japanese society. Everybody belongs to some kind of group, such as a company, a school, a neighborhood, or a hobby group. Since Japan is a crowed small country, good relationships among the group members are very important. The idea of giving *giri-choco* came from this atmosphere. The women in a group give a box of chocolates to their male bosses and colleagues. Everyone contributes so the chocolate is not from an individual. Usually each *giri-choco* costs just a couple of dollars for each woman. Often a Japanese woman spends an average of six dollars for obligation chocolate each year. In addition, they spend an average of twenty dollars for their real loved ones. Consequently, a chocolate company will sell more than 10% of its annual sales for Valentine's Day.

Another unique Japanese tradition is White Day. Japanese men cannot just receive the presents from women. Women also expect a return gift. On March 14, men should give marshmallows of white chocolate in return for the Valentine's Day *giri-choco* chocolate. Men have to prepare some sweets for their female colleagues as return gifts of Valentine's Day, so men have to spend quite a lot of money for this event. Women who give *honmei-choco* on Valentine's Day, expect a more serious gift in return. They expect to receive not only flowers or candies, but also jewelry or handbags on White Day.

Ideally, gift giving comes from the sender's heart. However, gift giving on Valentine's Day or White Day became a duty for Japanese workers. This idea originally came from a candy company in the 1970s. Both women and men think these customs are a waste of money, especially this obligation chocolate. Often recipients don't or can't eat all of these sweets, so they toss them away. These two days became very materialistic events. Only chocolate companies appreciate these customs. That's very sad. It contrasts greatly to the romantic celebration on Valentine's Day. I can still remember how I felt on my first Valentine's Day. It was real puppy love and sweet memories.

Valentine's Day in China
JUN XIA SHI

ON FEBRUARY 14, VALENTINE'S DAY, people send love messages or give something special to the people they love. It is a day many people around the world celebrate. In China, younger people celebrate this special occasion, too. They convey romance to their loved ones on this day. However, China has another Valentine's Day, a romantic day. It is the seventh day of the seventh lunar month on the Chinese calendar. We call the day Qixi, the night of sevens. There is a romantic love story behind this day. The seventh daughter of the Emperor of heaven and a poor orphaned cowherder fell in love. They got married and had two children together on Earth. The Emperor did not like this. He was very angry when he discovered the marriage. Then he separated them by creating the Milky Way Galaxy. The princess moved to the star Vega and the cowherder stayed on the star Altair. Once a year on the seventh night of the seventh moon, all the magpies in the world take pity on them and fly up into heaven to form a bridge over the star Deneb in the Cygus constellation so the lovers can be together. In remembrance of the story, people began to celebrate the seventh day of the seventh lunar month.

Hanami
YUKIKO EGAWA

HANAMI IS A JAPANESE CUSTOM. It is cherry blossom viewing and a picnic under the blooming trees. After a cold winter, people welcome a warm spring with Hanami. *Sakura*, cherry blossom in Japanese, is a symbol of the spring, and people love the blossoms. Almost every park in Japan has some cherry trees, and they bloom at the same time when the spring comes. They are very beautiful sights and almost magical. If people are walking through a row of cherry blossoms, they will be able to feel like they are in heaven. They can enjoy *sakura* only a couple of days in spring, so this blossom season is a very important and exciting time for Japanese.

When Sakura bloom, people have a picnic party with families, friends, or coworkers under the cherry blossoms. Some people sing and dance to express their joy. They drink sake, Japanese rice wine, or beer and eat a picnic lunch or dinner. Also, there is a special sweet for Hanami. It is called Hanami Dango, which is a piece of skewered dumplings. Each skewer has three different colored dumplings: white, pink, and green. Each color represents a season; white is the snow of the ending winter, pink is the color of the cherry blossom and the joy of spring, and green is the upcoming summer.

In Japan, Hanami season is held at the same time as the welcoming of the new employees in companies or the freshmen in universities. So, often they have Hanami as their welcome party. You can see that Japanese people really enjoy Hanami and celebrate spring surrounded by beautiful cherry blossoms. In addition, Hanami is a good occasion to communicate with the new employees or the new members of the group.

Adult Pledge Ceremony
ZIXIA LIU

IN CHINA, AN EIGHTEEN-YEAR-OLD IS an adult with adult responsibilities. An eighteen-year-old has legal responsibilities and obligations, driving privileges, drinking alcohol privileges, gambling privileges, and of course decision-making privileges. The eighteenth birthday is the most significant birthday for everyone born in China.

Most families have only one child in China. For families with only one child, that child's adulthood means a lot. It could mean less financial support. Sometimes young adults are ready to start work at this time. It could also mean the time to consider college. This means continued financial support and a greater commitment from the family. In my city, Canton, there is an important celebration, Adult Pledge Ceremony, to demonstrate the importance of becoming an adult.

The event was held in Sun-Yet-San Memorial Hall every year. High school students from all over the city gathered there for the ceremony. Now the population growth makes it necessary to have a ceremony in each high school. Still, this is an enormous honor and proud moment for every student in the ceremony.

I turned eighteen last June. I participated in the ceremony along with about 1,000 young adults. We were all quiet because of the grandeur of the ceremony. We were excited about being independent and sensible, but we were also nervous about the many responsibilities and obligations we would face. We focused on the director on stage and held onto the pledge pamphlet in our hands. The director said, "Please raise your right fists next to your temple." We all lifted our fists and opened our pamphlets. Following the director, we read the pledge out loud together. We read each sentence louder and louder. We could feel the power as well as the burden of adulthood. The words in the pamphlet seemed very powerful. At that moment, I felt ready to be an adult and to face my life with less and less help from my parents. I felt ready to accomplish my personal goals, to repay my parents and those who love me, to be genuine with trusted friends. At that moment we all grew up. We listened as we heard our names called out.

Then the principal gave a speech. The speeches varied every year, but the theme remained the same. He told about the meaning of adulthood, about the qualities of adulthood. He showed the difference between an adult and a teenager. He wanted us to understand the pressure that our parents feel. He motivated us to feel the fresh aspect of thinking like an adult.

An important part of Chinese culture is showing responsibility and gratitude to our parents. We want to repay our parents' love and effort in raising us. This ceremony gives new adults a time to think about their gratitude to their parents. It does not take long for this ceremony, perhaps only forty-five minutes. It is not complicated. We just read the pamphlet and listen to a speech. It is simple, but extremely important. It ceremonially announces a new group of adults.

Coming of Age Day
TAKESHI ISHII

WE JAPANESE HAVE MANY SPECIAL holidays and celebrations. These celebrations help people in society to connect with each other. Coming of Age Day, on the second Monday of January, is one of those. It is called Seijin-shiki in Japanese. Under Japanese law, at the age of twenty we become an adult, so people celebrate their becoming an adult with millions of other people every year. In Japan, there are several traditions for celebrating Seijin-shiki.

Clothes are very important for the young adults on Coming of Age Day. Young men usually wear a black suit, a white shirt, and a bright colorful tie. The tie shows individuality. Young women typically wear a *kimono*, traditional Japanese clothes. *Kimonos* have many colors and patterns like cherry blossoms and camellias. Young women also wear a favorite comb in their hair and carry a *kinchaku*, a traditional cloth purse. No woman looks the same in a *kimono*. They dress up to show they have become adults.

On the day of the celebration, young women and men gather at city halls, huge parks, or civic centers to hear a speech about adult responsibiltiy. This speech event is the most important part of Seijin-shiki. Some cities ask important people to give a speech or entertain the young adults. The entertainment could include shows, magic tricks, or comic dialogues. After the ceremony, people take photos with their family and friends. They also receive special gifts to honor them on this special day. In my case, I got a signet with my name carved in it. This represented my adult status. I was old enough to enter a legal contract.

In addition to those events, the young adults usually have a party later in the day with their friends. They go to bars or saloons after changing into casual clothes. They want to show other signs of adulthood. Now they are eligible to drink and smoke.

Seijin-shiki became popular after the Second World War when the Japanese Constitution was established. Under the constitution, twenty-year-olds are eligible to vote and that means adulthood. I am glad to have the memories of this celebration when I was twenty years old.

A Family Tradition
VICTORIA GONZALES

THE SAN FRANCISCO DE ASSISI celebration in my hometown, Tizapan, Jalisco, Mexico, is a long traditon. This religious celebration lasts for a full week with both praying and fun. Families gather for praying, music, bullfighting, fireworks, and a fair. The celebration begins on September 26 and continues until October 4 every year. We remember Saint Francis because he loved animals and nature.

The church and the merchants in town have a special association, and they begin the preparations for the celebration at least six months in advance. Volunteers are also welcome to participate. My family always participates in the Hijos Ausentes, the absent children. These are all the native people of Tizapan who do not live there anymore. This is a special activity so all of us can be part of the celebration. The memories of this are both happy and sad for me. They are happy because I remember my father and mother laughing and dancing with me. They are sad because my parents are not with me anymore.

The celebration includes a big praying fiesta. My knees hurt just thinking about the hours I spent on my knees praying. Activities at church begin at 5 AM with an hour of praying. Then the mariachi band arrives at church to sing Las Mananitas, like happy birthday to Saint Francis. Around 7 AM, breakfast is ready. All the residents bring traditional food to share. Then at 11 AM, we have a parade. We walk and greet our neighbors and friends. This is especially wonderful because we see many people. Sometimes we might see someone for the first time in many years. As we are walking and greeting our friends, the band continues to play music.

We all eventually arrive at the bullfighting arena. Many national and international bullfighting stars come for this celebration. The bullfighting events are always very exciting, but for some the addition of beer and tequila adds to the excitement.

Later in the evening, all residents gather for dinner. The town hosts this feast. It is like a family reunion for the entire town. I have a large family and many of them live far away. This celebration is our family reunion, too.

After dinner, everyone goes to see the fireworks. One very special one happens every year. We call it the castle because it resembles a big castle in the sky. It quickly blows into a million pieces and has a beautiful effect. Children and adults enjoy it very much. After the fireworks, we relax.

We sit at the plaza or walk around the plaza listening to music until midnight.

The San Francisco de Assisi celebration is one that brings family and friends together. My grandparents encouraged their children to participate, and my parents encouraged me. Now I am determined to maintain this tradition for my children and grandchildren.

 | Teacher's Guide

Using *One World Many Voices*

Both intensive and extensive reading are important aspects of an ESL reading curriculum. The essays in *One World Many Voices* are designed to provide interesting and easy extensive reading material. They can, however, be used effectively in many ways in the classroom. While extensive reading contributes to overall language proficiency growth and helps students to become successful readers, intensive reading provides instructor-led activities that help students develop reading proficiency and confidence.

Teachers can address factors that lead to unsuccessful and successful reading in the classroom through both intensive and extensive reading activities. Extensive reading alone will not remedy unsuccessful reading practices, but a combination of extensive reading and teacher-led intensive reading activities will remedy most.

FACTORS IN SUCCESSFUL AND UNSUCCESSFUL READING

Factors in Unsuccessful Reading
- Lack of rapid, automatic, and accurate word recognition
- Limited sight vocabulary
- Lack of phonological competence
- Limited grasp of the structure of the language
- Inability to disambiguate information in the text
- Inability to use reading strategies flexibly while reading
- Lack of general world knowledge
- Lack of interaction between textual and general world knowledge
- Rigidity in perception and conceptualization

 Teacher's Guide

Factors in Successful Reading
- Rapid, automatic, and accurate word recognition
- Large recognition vocabulary
- Reasonable grasp of the structure of the language
- Ability to disambiguate information
- Ability to establish a standard of coherence, monitor comprehension, set goals, and use strategies to reach that standard
- Ability to integrate meaning
- Ability to make inferences and connections to background knowledge
- Ability to suppress less important information
- Fluency in processing words, sentences, and discourse cues

EXTENSIVE READING

Extensive reading can help second language readers overcome some factors that lead to unsuccessful reading. Guided extensive reading programs provide readers with carefully selected material and suggestions for reading frequency. They promote reading fluency much the way that journal writing helps students become fluid writers. Most significantly, extensive reading provides reading practice. It guides time-on-task for readers who might not be self-motivated.

Material

In order to promote fluency, extensive reading material should be easy to read with few unfamiliar words and easy-to-process sentence structure. Students should be able to read faster than they read for intensive reading and should be encouraged not to use a dictionary. The purpose of extensive reading is general understanding.

Teacher's Guide

The essays in these collections are carefully edited for different proficiency levels of English learners. The vocabulary increases in breadth from the most frequent 500 words to the most frequent 2,000 words in English across the series. The sentence structure also increases in complexity over the collection.

The essays in *World Holidays* were edited for sentence structure and vocabulary to provide high-beginning level students with interesting and easy to read extensive reading material.

Each book in the series can provide a portion of the required extensive reading material for one semester. At every level of proficiency, students should engage in extensive reading four to five times a week in addition to the reading they do in class.

The Teacher's Role

Teachers can encourage, inspire, and motivate students to read by engaging in extensive reading along with their students in the classroom and by establishing an expectation of extensive reading outside of the classroom. Teachers are excellent models for reading and discussing books. They can share their own experiences with reading and tell students about the books they are reading. When teachers read the same books that the students are reading, they can share their reactions to the books and guide student discussions. Language learners often have limited experience reading in English or discussing things they read in their new language. The teacher can model these activities and encourage students to discuss their reading with each other.

Teachers might introduce extensive reading with activities that invite students to examine their reading experiences, habits, and attitudes toward reading in their first language.

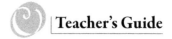 Teacher's Guide

Goals of Extensive Reading

Extensive reading can help second language readers overcome some factors that lead to unsuccessful reading practices. The goals of extensive reading include the following:

- Improve reading comprehension
- Increase rapid, automatic, and accurate recognition of the most frequent English words
- Encourage incidental vocabulary learning
- Increase reading rate
- Gain overall language proficiency
- Build general knowledge
- Support the development of a reader identity in English
- Establish a community of readers

Suggestions for Teacher-Directed Activities

The essays in *World Holidays* can be used as a classroom resource not only for extensive reading practice, but also for achieving overall reading goals. They are a resource for practicing reading skills and strategies that promote successful reading. The following suggestions have emerged from our experience using the essays in the classroom. We hope that you find them useful.

IMPROVE COMPREHENSION

Book discussions can help readers of English develop a sense of competence and autonomy as they read for comprehension. Discussion activities can help them monitor their comprehension and motivate them to develop comprehension strategies. Such strategies include re-reading, looking for key words or ideas, constructing mental summaries, and connecting ideas encountered in the text to their own experiences. Here are some activities that can help learners improve their comprehension.

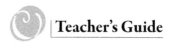

- After reading a passage once, tell a partner about the passage without looking at the text.
- Read a passage multiple times and tell a partner about the passage without looking at the text. Discuss the comprehension differences after a third or fourth reading.
- Connect the ideas in an essay to personal experience.
- Identify the main idea and supporting ideas of an essay.
- In pairs or small groups, discuss an essay in light of similarities and/or differences with personal experience.

LEARN AND PRACTICE READING STRATEGIES

Students learn reading strategies from their reading textbooks and practice applying those strategies during teacher-guided activities in class. The essays in this book can provide additional practice opportunities for mastering those strategies and for supporting their integration into students' independent reading practices. Here are some activities that can provide learners with opportunities to practice various reading strategies.

- Ask students to preview the book and discuss its overall organization as a class.
- After reading a chapter, ask students to work in pairs or small groups to draw inferences about one or more of the essays. For example, students might be asked to draw inferences about cultural expectations or values not explicitly discussed in an essay.
- Ask students to discuss their previous knowledge or experience with a topic from one of the chapters. For example, ask students to describe a New Year celebration in their culture or family.
- Ask students to scan for particular information. For example, students might scan a passage for key words or ideas.
- Select one essay in a chapter and ask students to look for transition signals, key words, or other coherence devices that link ideas from within and between paragraphs.

INCREASE READING RATE

Slow readers spend a great deal of time processing individual letters and words, making it difficult for them to understand what they are reading. Reading faster will aid comprehension and increase reading pleasure. It will also contribute to overall academic success. English language learners will naturally increase their reading speed over time as their general language proficiency increases, but with practice and guidance their reading speed can increase more quickly. Here are some activities that can help students increase their reading speed.

Reading Pairs
1. Select a passage from the book. Ask students to work with a partner.
2. Partner A reads aloud for 30 seconds.
3. Partner B reads the same passage for 30 seconds.
4. Repeat.
5. Ask how many more words were read each time.

Reading Sprints
1. Select a passage from the book. Ask students to read silently for four minutes. Use a timer or a watch with a second hand. Then ask them to count the number of lines they read.
2. Students then count out the same number of lines in the next part of the passage. They continue reading for three minutes, trying to read the same number of lines in less time. Students count the lines they read in three minutes, count out the same number of lines in the next part of the passage, and try to read as many lines in two minutes.
3. When the reading sprint is complete, the class can discuss their comprehension of the text.

Monitor
1. Encourage students to monitor their reading speed.
2. Have students chart their progress.

 Teacher's Guide

RAPID, ACCURATE, AUTOMATIC WORD RECOGNITION
Increased reading comprehension and reading speed are only possible when students can rapidly and accurately recognize large numbers of words in print. Their vocabulary for listening and speaking is not accessed for reading unless they also recognize what a word looks like on the printed page and then connect that word to their mental lexicon. Extensive reading exposes language learners to the printed word, but it does not ensure that students accurately process the correct meaning. Some read aloud activities can help language learners connect printed words to the vocabulary they have developed for listening and speaking. It can also provide consistent pronunciation practice.

Read Aloud
- After students read a passage silently twice, ask them to read it aloud to a partner.
- Assign one paragraph of a passage to each student. For homework the student should practice reading aloud, focusing on careful pronunciation and phrasing. In class, students read to each other.

Pronunciation
- Encourage students to use the computer software or Internet interface of an English language learner dictionary and ensure that students know the pronunciation of the a large number of the most frequent English words.
- Encourage students to say and write words to promote the connection between the written and spoken forms.
- Make pronunciation an important part of knowing a word.

 Teacher's Guide

ENCOURAGE INCIDENTAL LEARNING AND DEEPEN WORD KNOWLEDGE

Sometimes students believe that reading will help their vocabulary development only if reading texts contain many new words. Talking to students about the value of reading easy texts for learning vocabulary may help them see the value of extensive reading more clearly.

Extensive reading can also help students deepen their knowledge of known words since knowing a word includes many types of knowledge such as knowing the spelling, pronunciation, and multiple meanings of the word. Simple activities such as reading aloud, listening and repeating, and listening to audio files of passages can all contribute to deepening learners' knowledge of a word. Teachers can also direct students' attention to words in a passage that draw on less frequent uses of those words.

LINK READING AND WRITING

Regular journal writing about topics from their reading can promote both reading and writing fluency. Ungraded reflective writing about their ideas after reading promotes close reading, encourages readers to explore reactions to the text, gives them a chance to examine features of a text more closely, and encourages readers to link their own experiences to those of the writer. Here are some possible journal prompts.

- What does the author mean by...?
- How are the experiences of the authors different from or similar to your experiences?
- What did you think about as you read...?
- What was interesting/confusing about this essay/chapter?
- Write about your own favorite holiday celebration.

 **Teacher's Guide**

INCREASE OVERALL LANGUAGE PROFICIENCY

Listening, speaking, reading, and writing in English all require knowledge of grammar. Reading easy and interesting material, as students do with extensive reading, helps them confirm their knowledge of English grammar and provides extensive input upon which to make further generalizations about English grammar. Here are some activity types that can help learners gain overall language proficiency.

Sound-Spelling Relationship

- A student whose native language uses a writing system that is very different from the English alphabet will likely benefit from activities that focus attention on sound-spelling relationships.
- Copying a paragraph can give students easy practice with forming letters and spelling.

Grammar Analysis

Analyzing the grammar in a passage helps students to focus on language structure and to discuss their observations. Each activity should take no more than 15 minutes. The possibilities are endless, but here are some ideas.

1. First, select a paragraph that has a sufficient number of the target structure and make an overhead transparency of the paragraph.
2. Students should first work alone for three minutes to identify as many examples of the target structure as they can.
3. Next, ask students to work in pairs to confirm their findings.
4. Finally show your own findings on the overhead. At the high-beginning level, students benefit from identifying the subjects, verbs, and objects. They can identify noun phrases, prepositional phrases, subject phrases, and verb phrases. They can find pronouns and referents, gerunds and infinitives, and articles. They can also begin to make generalizations about articles by observing them in the text.

 **Teacher's Guide**

DEVELOP FLUENCY

Reading fluency and speaking fluency often develop at different rates. When students have opportunities to talk about what they are reading, they bring together multiple skills. The activities below also encourage integrating reading and speaking skills as well as multiple readings of a text, which can deepen understanding and enable readers to see something new with each reading.

Read Aloud

Students should read a passage silently multiple times and rehearse before reading it aloud to a partner.

Oral Summaries

Students retell passages from memory and confirm comprehension.

1. Students read one entry as many times as they can for 10 – 12 minutes.
2. With a partner, retell/summarize the passage.
3. Identify key points with the whole class.
4. Read the passage again.

Summary Sprints

In pairs, students summarize a passage.

1. Student A has three minutes to summarize the passage.
2. Student B has two minutes to summarize the same passage.
3. Student A has one minute to summarize the same passage.

 | **Teacher's Guide**

BUILD GENERAL KNOWLEDGE

Each chapter in *World Holidays* includes both personal experience and information about the writer's culture. This diversity of experiences provides geographical, cultural, religious, and family perspectives and provides an opportunity for readers to develop knowledge about holidays in different cultures and countries that are very different from their own. They can confirm their new knowledge through discussion activities or research assignments.

ENGAGE IN CRITICAL THINKING

Students need practice thinking and analyzing as they read. Some simple activities that encourage students to think about organization of ideas and how ideas relate across several essays can help students to do this on their own. Here are some examples of how to use the book to encourage critical thinking.

- Each chapter in the book focuses on a particular type of holiday. Select several passages about the same holiday, and ask students to work in small groups to identify similarities and differences.
- Encourage students to draw conclusions from reading about a particular type of holiday. Ask critical thinking questions such as why a particular holiday was important to the author, what aspects of the holiday celebration reveal something about the author's culture, or what the author does not express that might be important.
- Ask students to select their favorite essay from a given chapter and to tell a group of students the reasons for their opinions.

 | **Teacher's Guide**

SUPPORT READER IDENTITY IN ENGLISH

Developing an identity as an English reader over the course of several semesters can help language learners transition from learning to read to reading to learn. Extensive reading provides the time-on-task that builds confidence, promotes learning, and provides practice. All of these can lead to increased pleasure reading, other types of independent reading, and related oral or written activities that readers engage in as part of what it means to be a reader. Activities that invite students to discuss or write about their experiences as English readers can help them be more aware of their development of an English reader identity.

CREATE A COMMUNITY OF READERS

Many of us have had the pleasurable experience of talking to friends and colleagues about a book we have read. When we discuss our own reading with others, we become part of a larger community of readers. When language learners engage in reading the same book as part of their extensive reading, they have the opportunity to experience that same pleasure. They share their ideas and participate in a community that values reading and sharing ideas about that reading.

Countries

AFGHANISTAN
ARMENIA
BRAZIL
BULGARIA
BURMA
CAMBODIA
CHINA
COLOMBIA
CURACAO
EL SALVADOR
INDIA
INDONESIA
IRAN
JAPAN
KOREA
MALI
MEXICO
MONGOLIA
NICARAGUA
PERU
POLAND
RUSSIA
TAIWAN
THAILAND
UKRAINE
VIETNAM

AUTHOR	Essay Title & Year	Page Number
Alfaro, Maria	Mother's Day in Colombia 2009	55
Alvarado, Saida	Indian's Day in Peru 2006	46
Alvarez, Ana	Virgin of Guadalupe, Mexico 2006	79
Anonymous	Brazilian New Year Traditions 2007	9
Anonymous	Norooz in Afghanistan 2006	14
Anonymous	Pchum Ben Festival 2007	62
Beltar, Maria Elena	Independence Day in Mexico 2006	101
Budiman, Victoria	Chinese New Year in Indonesia 2006	22
Chang, Bernard	A Holiday in my Native Country, China 2006	52
Chunyu, Kina	Bathing the Buddha Festival 2006	73
Dittmann, Alina	Saint Andrew's Day Eve in Poland 2007	112
Egawa, Yukiko	Shichi-Go-San 2009	49
Egawa, Yukiko	Hanami 2009	120
Egawa, Yukiko	Valentine's Day in Japan 2010	117
Esparza, Javier	A Parade and Fireworks 2006	102
Farooqi, Jamila	Eid 2006	69
Fransindani, Edward	Independence Day in Indonesia 2006	108
Gong, Yang Xing	The Dragon Boat Festival 2006	54
Gonzales, Victoria	A Family Tradition 2007	124
He, Pingfan	Mid-Autumn Festival in China 2006	32
Hirsch, Angela	Lantern Festival in Taiwan 2006	36
Ishii, Takeshi	Coming of Age Day 2009	123
Joya, Maritza	Christmas in Colombia 2006	85
Keita, Moulaye C.	Mali Independence 2009	107
Kelling, Sandra	Festa Junina in Brazil 2006	75
Khosravan, Mojdeh	A Persian Holiday 2006	12
Kim, Kyung-Jin	Thank You, Teachers in Korea 2006	51
Krogh, Somthawin	Loy Krathong 2006	41
Lam, Keung	A Unique Chinese Holiday, Ching Ming 2006	57
Lauer, Yana	Christmas in Ukraine 2007	96
Lee, Yejin	Sol-nal in Korea 2006	27
Lee, Suson	Chuseok with My Husband's Family 2006	37
Li, Andrew	The Most Important Chinese Holiday 2006	19
Liu, Pin C.	Tomb Sweeping Day 2009	59
Liu, Yu Jie	Being Together 2006	35

Index of Authors

AUTHOR	Essay Title & Year	Page Number
Liu, Yu Jie	Chung Yang Festival 2007	115
Liu, Zixia	Adult Pledge Ceremony 2009	121
Manoukian, Arsineh	Trendez, an Armenian Tradition 2006	74
Marquis, Marilyn	Federal Holidays Honoring People 2009	44
Marquis, Marilyn	Days of the Dead 2009	64
Marquis, Marilyn	My Christmas Memories 2007	92
Martinez, Deysi M	Christmas in El Salvador 2006	88
Massen, Vanessa	Cambodia's Water Festival 2006	39
Mitchum, Nuru	Banda Bou Day in Curaçao 2006	105
Morris, Elena	The New Year in Russia 2006	11
Mungunkhuyag, Mendjargal	Tsagaan Sar in Mongolia 2006	21
Nguyen, Hoa	Lunar New Year 2006	23
Nielsen, Sarah	New Year Celebrations 2007	8
Nielsen, Sarah	My Mid-Autumn Festival Tradition 2007	30
Nielsen, Sarah	July 4th Memories 2007	99
Ortiz, Martha	When Christmas Begins 2006	89
Ponce de Leon, Narda Diaz	Celebrate with Feelings 2006	103
Sarmiento-Achulli, Ruth	A Unique Tradition in My Family 2007	78
Shein, Yin Yin	Christmas in Burma 2006	84
Shi, Jun Xia	Valentine's Day in China 2009	119
Smirnova, Viktoriya	Pancake Week in Russia 2009	114
Srinivasan, Kalyani	Pongal Festival 2006	110
Summers, Jennifer	Christmas in Nicaragua 2006	90
Susie, Yun	The Korean Death Ceremony 2007	60
Takashima, Yukiko	Children's Day in Japan 2006	48
Torres, Jose	Dia De Los Muertos 2007	67
Tran, Vy	The Excitement of Tet 2006	24
Trika, Novieda	Eid Al Fitr in Indonesia 2006	71
Uramatsu, Kyoko	Obon: When Spirits Return 2007	61
Valdez, Juan	Day of the Dead in Mexico 2009	65
Vasquez, Julia	The New Year in Peru 2006	10
Waldman, Terumi	Hina Matsuri In Japan 2006	47
Yossifova, Nadejda	Christmas in Bulgaria 2006	82
Zhang, Hong	The Most Popular Festival 2006	17

About the Editors

*M*ARILYN MARQUIS TEACHES ESL AT Las Positas College in Livermore, California. She was inspired to become an ESL teacher after hosting two young people through the Experiment in International Living. She began teaching English as a Second Language at Long Beach City College in 1983. She was an adjunct English and ESL teacher there until 1991 when she joined the faculty at Las Positas College. Reading instruction has been an area of particular interest to her throughout her professional life. She has enjoyed the collaboration on this series of student-generated essays. Marilyn holds a bachelor's degree in English from California State University, Northridge and a master's degree from California State University, Dominguez Hills.

*S*ARAH NIELSEN HAS BEEN INTERESTED in language learning and teaching since she was a high school student. She spent a year in Belgium living with a French speaking family and attending school before she began her university education. She taught English in China for two years before entering graduate school. She began teaching as an adjunct ESL instructor in 1995 before joining the faculty at Las Positas College in 2000. In 2004, she joined the faculty at California State University, East Bay, as the coordinator of the MA TESOL program. Sarah holds a bachelor's degree from the University of California, Santa Cruz, and both a master's degree, and a Ph.D. from the University of California, Davis.

CPSIA information can be obtained
at www.ICGtesting.com
Printed in the USA
BVHW08s1814130818
524264BV00002B/156/P